DATE DUE			

3 4026 00242229 8
Carlson, Janet F.

Personality and
abnormal psychology

SHEPARD MIDDLE SCHOOL

Student Handbook to Psychology

Personality and Abnormal Psychology

Volume VI

Student Handbook to Psychology

Personality and Abnormal Psychology

Volume VI

JANET F. CARLSON

Bernard C. Beins
General Editor

Facts On File
An Infobase Learning Company

Student Handbook to Psychology: Personality and Abnormal Psychology
Copyright © 2012 Janet F. Carlson

Facts On File, Inc.
An Imprint of Infobase Learning
132 West 31st Street
New York NY 10001

Library of Congress Cataloging-in-Publication Data
Student handbook to psychology / [edited by] Bernard C. Beins.
    v. ; cm.
  Includes bibliographical references and index.
  Contents: v. 1. History, perspectives, and applications / Kenneth D. Keith—v. 2. Methods and measurements / Bernard C. Beins—v. 3. Brain and mind / Michael Kerchner—v. 4. Learning and thinking / Christopher M. Hakala and Bernard C. Beins—v. 5. Developmental psychology / Lynn Shelley—v. 6. Personality and abnormal psychology / Janet F. Carlson—v. 7. Social psychology / Jeffrey D. Holmes and Sheila K. Singh.
  ISBN 978-0-8160-8280-3 (set : alk. paper)—ISBN 978-0-8160-8281-0 (v. 1 : alk. paper)—ISBN 978-0-8160-8286-5 (v. 2 : alk. paper)—ISBN 978-0-8160-8285-8 (v. 3 : alk. paper)—ISBN 978-0-8160-8284-1 (v. 4 : alk. paper)—ISBN 978-0-8160-8282-7 (v. 5 : alk. paper)—ISBN 978-0-8160-8287-2 (v. 6 : alk. paper)—ISBN 978-0-8160-8283-4 (v. 7 : alk. paper) 1. Psychology—Textbooks.
I. Beins, Bernard.
  BF121.S884 2012
  150—dc23   2011045277

Text design by Erika K. Arroyo
Cover design by Takeshi Takahashi
Composition by EJB Publishing Services
Cover printed by Yurchak Printing, Landisville, Pa.
Book printed and bound by Yurchak Printing, Landisville, Pa.
Date printed: September 2012
Printed in the United States of America

This book is printed on acid-free paper.

CONTENTS

PREFACE

Behavior is endlessly fascinating. People and other animals are complicated creatures that show extraordinary patterns of abilities, intelligence, social interaction, and creativity along with, unfortunately, problematic behaviors. All of these characteristics emerge because of the way the brain interprets incoming information and directs our responses to that information.

This seven-volume **Student Handbook to Psychology** set highlights important and interesting facets of thought and behavior. It provides a solid foundation for learning about psychological processes associated with growth and development, social issues, thinking and problem solving, and abnormal thought and behavior. Most of the major schools and theories related to psychology appear in the books in the series, albeit in abbreviated form. Because psychology is such a highly complex and diverse discipline, these volumes present a broad overview of the subject rather than a complete and definitive treatise. Such a work, in fact, would be difficult (if not impossible) because psychological scientists are still searching for answers to a great number of questions. If you are interested in delving in more depth into specific areas of psychology, we have provided a bibliography of accessible readings to help you fill in the details.

The volumes in this series follow the order that you might see in a standard presentation on a variety of topics, but each book stands alone and the series does not need to be read in any particular order. In fact, you can peruse individual chapters in each volume at will, seeking out and focusing on those topics that interest you most. On the other hand, if you do choose to read through a complete volume, you will find a flow of information that connects related sections of the books, providing a coherent overview of the entire discipline of psychology.

The authors of the seven volumes in this series are experts in their respective fields, so you will find psychological concepts that are up to date and that reflect the most recent advances in scientific knowledge about thought and behavior. In addition, each of the authors is an excellent writer who has presented the information in an interesting and compelling fashion. Although some of the material and many of the ideas are complex, the authors have done an outstanding job of conveying those ideas in ways that are both interesting and effective.

In *History, Perspectives, and Applications*, Professor Kenneth Keith of the University of San Diego has woven historical details into a tapestry that shows how psychological questions originated within a philosophical framework, incorporated biological concepts, and ultimately evolved into a single scientific discipline that remains interconnected with many other academic and scientific disciplines. Dr. Keith has identified the major figures associated with the development of the field of psychology as well as the social forces that helped shape their ideas.

In *Methods and Measurements*, I illustrate how psychologists create new knowledge through research. The volume presents the major approaches to research and explains how psychologists develop approaches to research that help us answer questions about complex aspects of behavior. Without these well-structured and proven research methods, we would not have much of the information we now have about behavior. Furthermore, these methods, approaches, and practices provide confidence that the knowledge we do have is good knowledge, grounded in solid research.

Many people are under the impression that each thought or behavior is a single thing. In *Brain and Mind*, Professor Michael Kerchner of Washington College dispels this impression by showing how the myriad structures and functions of our brain work in unison to create those seemingly simple and one-dimensional behaviors. As the author explains, each behavior is really the result of many different parts of the brain engaging in effective communication with one another. Professor Kerchner also explains what occurs when this integration breaks down.

Learning and Thinking, co-authored by Professor Christopher Hakala of Western New England College and me (at Ithaca College), explores the fascinating field of cognitive psychology, a discipline focused on the processes by which people learn, solve problems, and display intelligence. Cognitive psychology is a fascinating field that explores how we absorb information, integrate it, and then act on it.

In *Developmental Psychology*, Professor Lynn Shelley of Westfield State University addresses the very broad area of psychology that examines how people develop and change from the moment of conception through old age. Dr. Shelley's detailed and compelling explanation includes a focus on how maturation and environment play a part in shaping how each individual grows, evolves, and changes.

In *Personality and Abnormal Psychology*, Professor Janet Carlson of the Buros Center for Testing at the University of Nebraska (Lincoln) addresses various dimensions of personality, highlighting processes that influence normal and abnormal facets of personality. Dr. Carlson also explains how psychologists study the fundamental nature of personality and how it unfolds.

The final volume in this series is *Social Psychology*. Co-authored by Professor Jeffrey Holmes of Ithaca College and Sheila Singh of Cornell University, this volume examines how our thoughts and behaviors emerge in connection with our interactions with other people. As the authors of this volume explain, changes in a person's social environment can lead to notable changes in the way that person thinks and behaves.

As editor of this series, I have had the opportunity to work with all of the authors who have contributed their expertise and insights to this project. During this collaborative process, I found that we have much in common. All of us have spent our careers pondering why people think and act the way they do. For every answer we come up with, we also develop new questions that are just as interesting and important. And we all agree that you cannot find a more interesting subject to study than psychology.

As you learn about psychology, we hope that the information in these seven volumes inspires the same fascination in you. We also hope that our explanations, illustrations, and narrative studies motivate you to continue studying why we humans are the way we are.

—Bernard C. Beins, Ph.D., Professor of Psychology,
Ithaca College, Series Editor

CHAPTER 1

UNDERSTANDING PERSONALITY

Personality serves as the lens through which we view and interpret the world and events within that world. It leads us to act in a largely predictable and consistent manner. The consistency we witness in other people's actions and views helps us to forge relationships with others that we value and upon which we can depend.

When we try to understand another person, we often rely upon what we know about how that person looks upon and interacts with the world. If we try to anticipate someone's reaction to an event, we again may use our knowledge of that person's overall demeanor or previous responses to similar events. For example, we expect someone we regard as optimistic to respond in a manner consistent with his or her optimistic tendency—to see the bright side of events or situations.

NATURE OF PERSONALITY

Enduring characteristics demonstrated by individuals make up what we call **personality**. The pattern of characteristics an individual displays tends to be stable across time and across a variety of situations. Thus, features of one's personality that become evident during childhood continue to exist as the child matures. For example, a child who shows compassion towards animals likely will grow into an adult who demonstrates a caring attitude towards animals.

Ordinarily, we describe someone's personality with more than one adjective. This approach makes sense, because an individual's personality tends to

Children who show compassion towards animals tend to grow into adults with a caring attitude towards animals. *(Shutterstock)*

be multifaceted. For example, a compassionate person also may be energetic, serene, patient, resourceful, self-reliant, obstinate, resolute, resilient, conscientious, miserly, and so forth. Moreover, the circumstances surrounding a given individual influence which part of his or her personality we see. For example, a weary traveler who arrives at his or her hotel only to find a room is not yet ready might show patience by taking a seat in the lobby and, perhaps, reading a book to pass the time. Another weary travel who encounters the same set of circumstances may show impatience by standing at the check-in counter and asking the front desk clerk every minute or two about the room's availability.

MAJOR FRAMEWORKS

The collection of characteristics that individuals possess distinguishes people from one another. Each collection of features represents a unique assemblage. All the major frameworks for understanding personality agree with this basic premise. The perspectives differ primarily in terms of their stance regarding the source, essential composition, and development of one's characteristics. Major sources of influence include biology, experience, phenomenology (humanism), and unconscious events. The following discussion summarizes the major frameworks for understanding personality that derive from these varied sources of influence.

Trait Theories (Biological Perspective)

Although each group of personal qualities that individuals possess represents a unique assemblage, collections may resemble one another. Furthermore, groups of characteristics may contain similar elements that are recognizable—arguably across all individuals. As an analogy, think about bouquets of flowers. Each individual flower represents a single characteristic or trait (e.g., arrogance, devotion, loyalty). An entire bouquet represents an entire collection of characteristics, similar to the group of traits an individual person possesses.

We know a bouquet of flowers when we see one, although there are endless possible combinations of flowers that may comprise a bouquet. The same idea applies to personality and the individual traits comprising a given personality. Flower bouquets vary in size and composition, as some contain a greater assortment of flower types than others. Some kinds of flowers rarely appear in bouquets (e.g., Venus flytrap) just as certain traits appear rarely in personality (e.g., despotism). And we find some bouquets—and some personalities—more attractive than others.

Personality psychologists who subscribe to the general line of thought described above believe personality is best described by traits. **Traits** are dimensions of personality. People do not differ in terms of whether or not they possess a given trait. Rather, people vary in terms of how much of a given trait they possess. Trait theorists contend that there are a finite number of traits and expend little effort to identify the sources of traits. Like physical characteristics (e.g., eye color and height), personality characteristics simply exist and most likely result from the biological blueprint provided in our genetic code.

How traits come to exist is far less important to trait theorists than what traits exist and which ones constitute superordinate traits. Thus, much of the research conducted in this area attempts to discern the essential dimensions of personality. As an analogy, think about the three colors used to create visual displays on a standard television screen or computer monitor: red, green, and blue. All colors observed on the screen or monitor can be reduced to (understood as) a combination of varying levels of these three essential colors. In much the same way, trait theorists have sought to identify the essential ingredients that can be combined in varying amounts to yield every imaginable personality.

What are the essential elements of personality? The answer depends on which trait theorist one asks. Personality psychologists credit Gordon Allport as the founder of trait theory. Allport's efforts began with an extensive review of words in an unabridged dictionary. He searched for terms that could be applied to personality and identified many thousands (about 4,500) of these descriptors.

Allport then streamlined his approach by suggesting three basic categories of traits: cardinal, central, and secondary. The categories differ in terms of salience. **Cardinal traits** are best considered as singular, defining characteristics. Few people possess cardinal traits. Such traits are so pervasive that they overshadow all other traits.

Central traits represent the primary qualities of an individual. You probably would use these kinds of traits to describe a person you know reasonably well. If asked to do so, you might describe the person as trustworthy, efficient, sociable, ebullient, affable, and compliant. By describing the person in this way, you have captured the essence of that individual. Most often, people describe themselves or other people with between five and ten central traits.

Secondary traits influence behavior in more circumscribed ways than central or cardinal traits. They may not be apparent except under specific situations. Secondary traits are far less salient than either central traits or, obviously, cardinal traits. To describe a person you know reasonably well, you may mention a secondary trait or two almost by accident. For example, after describing the person as generous, gracious, gentle, gregarious, and affectionate, you might add "and she loves to make puns."

Another approach to specifying essential traits involves reducing the total number of possible traits to a more manageable number by applying the statistical technique of **factor analysis**. In the context of personality, factor analysis uses statistical indicators of association among traits to group together those traits that go together. Factor analysis uses numerical evidence to establish how many factors exist within a given set of variables. The procedure reduces a larger number of traits to a smaller number of factors. For example, instead of considering 10 separate traits that bear a relationship to one another, a single overarching factor can be used to summarize and convey the same information.

Mother Teresa of Calcutta demonstrated a cardinal trait of humanitarianism. *(Photo by Tim Graham/Getty)*

Personality psychologist Raymond Cattell used factor analytic techniques to identify 16 basic dimensions of personality. A pair of traits, which Cattell termed **source traits**, anchors each dimension. An individual's personality can be quantified on each of the 16 dimensions, using a personality inventory that Cattell developed: the Sixteen Personality Factor Questionnaire, or 16 PF.

Hans Eysenck also employed factor analysis to distill the basic dimensions of personality. However, Eysenck concluded that personality consisted of just three major factors: extraversion, neuroticism, and psychoticism. **Extraversion** refers to one's degree of sociability. **Neuroticism** refers to one's level of emotional stability. **Psychoticism** refers to the degree to which one distorts reality. Combinations of just these three dimensions of personality produce a large variety of unique personalities.

Another trait approach to personality used factor analytic techniques to identify key personality traits. Among personality psychologists, a growing consensus surrounds the utility of what has come to be called the "Big Five" personality factors: openness to experience, conscientiousness, extraversion, agreeableness, and neuroticism.

These five factors have emerged consistently from factor analyses conducted with different populations within and outside of the United States. Because of the extensive research base that supports the **five-factor model** (FFM) of personality, the Big Five (or FFM) dominates as the most influential trait theory today.

TABLE 1.1
The "Big Five" Factors of Personality (OCEAN)

Dimension (trait factors)	Description
Openness to experience	Willingness or tendency to engage in novel and varied experiences; welcoming of varied perspectives; curious
Conscientiousness	Organized, efficient, self-disciplined; tendency to engage in planned activity; tendency to achieve or complete goal
Extraversion	Outgoing and energetic; tendency to seek company and to derive stimulation from association with others
Agreeableness	Cooperative; sympathetic to needs of others; friendly
Neuroticism	Sensitive; vulnerable; tendency towards unpleasant emotions (e.g., anger, depression, anxiety)

Learning Theories (Experiential Perspective)

Personality may be conceptualized as the result of biologically based traits, as trait theorists suggest. That, however, is only one view. Other personality psychologists argue that biology has little or no relationship to personality. Instead, personality develops over time as a function of our experiences and interactions with the world around us and our responses or interpretations of these events. A number of personality theorists employ this type of experiential framework to explain the process that establishes our unique personalities.

The most basic of these experiential theories, behaviorism, suggests that an individual's personality derives from the compilation of his or her behaviors across time. Patterns of behaviors come to exist because of repeated patterns of environmental events that accompany or follow particular behaviors. Learning theorists who fully embrace the tenets of associative and consequential learning assert that behaviors develop entirely because of environmental events that either co-occur with them or follow them.

According to **classical learning** (conditioning) theory, a neutral (i.e., meaningless) environmental event that occurs repeatedly at the same time as a given behavior establishes an association between the behavior and the event. After a number of repetitions, the previously meaningless event becomes meaning-*ful*. As a simple example, think about a doorbell that rings. There is nothing inherently meaningful about the sound a doorbell makes. But the sound of the doorbell comes to mean that someone is at the door, because the sound and presence of visitors are paired (repeatedly) in our experience. Our dogs learn this association rather quickly, too!

Another way that experience shapes behavior and, ultimately, personality derives from **operant learning** (conditioning) paradigms and involves what happens after we demonstrate a particular behavior. If what follows an emitted behavior constitutes a welcome reward, the behavior likely will be repeated in the future. If what follows is something neutral or negative, the behavior probably will not be repeated. For example, if a child receives a cookie each time he or she shares toys with a playmate, that child will be inclined to repeat the behavior (of sharing). If rewards continue to follow the behavior (i.e., the behavior is positively reinforced), sharing will become a behavioral pattern. The same kind of system of environmental consequences would produce all other aspects of the child's personality (e.g., resourcefulness, patience, resilience, gregariousness).

Some personality theorists find it rather difficult to apply strict learning principles to human behaviors. After all, many human behaviors are far more complicated than merely connecting the idea that the sound of a doorbell signals a visitor at the door. The sheer number of behaviors that humans demonstrate makes it hard to imagine that they all could develop according to learning principles. Moreover, some behaviors appear to have no basis in prior associations or patterns of "rewards." How are these behaviors established?

Social cognitive approaches to personality may provide an answer. Julian Rotter and Albert Bandura developed ideas about how people learn behaviors within the social context of their environments. Initially, Rotter suggested that the response to an exhibited behavior influences the motivation one has to exhibit the behavior again. People seek to achieve positive outcomes and to avoid negative ones. So far, this description aligns with the basic ideas of learning theory. But Rotter added the idea of **expectancies**—a cognitive phenomenon—to his theory of social learning. Specifically, Rotter held that if one expects a positive outcome to result from a given behavior (or believes there is a high probability of one) then one is more likely to engage in that given behavior.

Rotter also applied the concept of **locus of control** to describe how people differ in their beliefs about the extent to which they control events that impact them. People who believe that events control them have a high external locus (Latin for "location") of control. Such people believe that events happen to them because of the actions of powerful others or simply because of fate or happenstance. On the other hand, people who believe that they control events have a high internal locus of control. Such people believe that most events happen because of their own actions. People with a high internal locus of control act accordingly—they take action politically more often than people with a high external locus of control, and they believe their actions (e.g., attempts to influence others) will be successful.

Albert Bandura elaborated on Rotter's ideas. He believed that human behavior results from a complex interaction of events taking place in the environment and our inner experiences. As the label implies, social cognitive approaches address interpersonal and thinking processes as part of the learning model in order to explain how personality develops. As a type of learning theory, social cognitive theories assert that people acquire new behaviors and new knowledge by observing the actions of other people. Oftentimes, the behaviors of interest involve social behaviors (e.g., altruism, gratitude, aggression). These theories emphasize the importance of cognitive elements of human existence—thoughts, expectations, and feelings—in shaping personality.

Imitation occurs when one repeats behavior that one has observed another person perform. Imitation is also called **observational learning**, **social modeling**, and **vicarious learning**. All of these terms refer to situations wherein a behavior is established (learned) in one person who simply watches (observes) another person perform the action. According to social cognitive approaches, it is not necessary for an observer to experience directly any consequences of a particular behavior—merely seeing another person engage in the behavior may be enough to establish the behavior in the observer. For example, a toddler often repeats words he or she hears a parent utter—even (much to the parent's chagrin) four-letter words that he or she heard only once.

Imitation is not absolute, however. One simply does not imitate all behaviors one sees. In fact, an individual who observes a specific behavior may demonstrate a different behavior altogether. He or she may think about the observed action in terms of his or her own feelings and values or may have gained contrasting knowledge from witnessing the actions of another. For example, witnessing another person's attempts to solve a visual puzzle may help one learn what does not work (i.e., what not to do). If asked to solve the same visual puzzle, the observer will not imitate behaviors that did not lead to a solution but is likely to demonstrate other behaviors in attempting to solve the puzzle.

People may fail to imitate the actions of another person for other reasons, too. There are several steps that must be in place for imitation to occur. In brief, one must see the behavior of interest, pay attention to it, remember it, and then demonstrate it. If an observer does not pay attention or does not retain the action performed, he or she will not be able to demonstrate the behavior, even after seeing it happen. In addition, the person must be motivated to display the behavior. In other words, there must be a good reason to want to adopt the behavior.

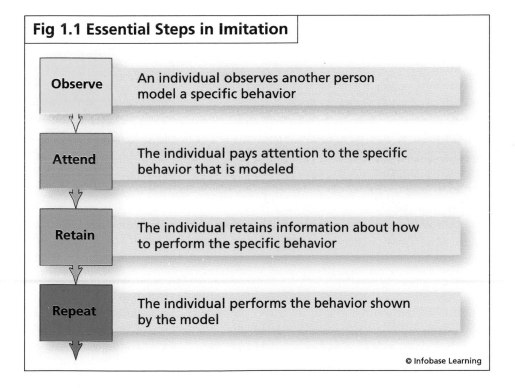

Fig 1.1 Essential Steps in Imitation

Observe	An individual observes another person model a specific behavior
Attend	The individual pays attention to the specific behavior that is modeled
Retain	The individual retains information about how to perform the specific behavior
Repeat	The individual performs the behavior shown by the model

© Infobase Learning

Consistent with traditional learning theorists, Bandura believed that behaviors must be reinforced if they are to be maintained. He identified three types of reinforcement. **External reinforcement** is the overt consequence of a demonstrated behavior. **Vicarious reinforcement** represents an indirect experience of reinforcement. It occurs when an observer watches a model receive a consequence for demonstrating a particular behavior. The observer experiences the consequence vicariously (through the experience of another). **Self-reinforcement** is a consequence delivered to oneself, by oneself, for demonstrating a particular behavior.

Bandura's model addresses at least a portion of the complicated reality of human existence. He recognized that people have the capacity to think and feel and developed a theory that accounted for these human factors. Bandura proposed that internal, cognitive events (e.g., thoughts, feelings, expectations, and values) and external, environmental events affect each other, a viewpoint known as **reciprocal determinism**. Our cognitive processes allow us to shape and influence our environment and to interpret and organize events that occur within it. Because we possess such high-level cognitive abilities, we can anticipate the consequences of our actions and use this knowledge to choose how we interact with the environment and the people in it.

Humanistic Theories (Phenomenological Perspective)

Another major personality perspective centers on the idea of people's innate goodness and tendency to develop in healthy and positive directions. The humanistic perspective emphasizes the worth of humans as individuals, as well as their values, interests, and welfare. Theorists from this perspective hold that human beings naturally grow in ways that help us to reach and fulfill our potential.

The humanistic perspective represents a markedly different approach to personality than traditional viewpoints such as psychodynamic (e.g., Freudian) or learning approaches. Personality psychologists who subscribe to a humanistic view assert that we do not need any sort of external motivator or reward to follow a healthy, positive, personally fulfilled trajectory of development. We enter the world fully equipped with the potential to thrive and, under ordinary conditions, make natural choices that move us toward the fulfillment of our potential.

Abraham Maslow introduced the idea of motivation to achieve self-fulfillment as a naturally occurring phenomenon. Maslow's early work attempted to explain human motivation, rather than personality. He described a **hierarchy of needs** in which people sought to satisfy their most basic needs—for example, physiological needs such as food, water, and sleep—before seeking the satisfaction of higher level needs, such as self-esteem needs.

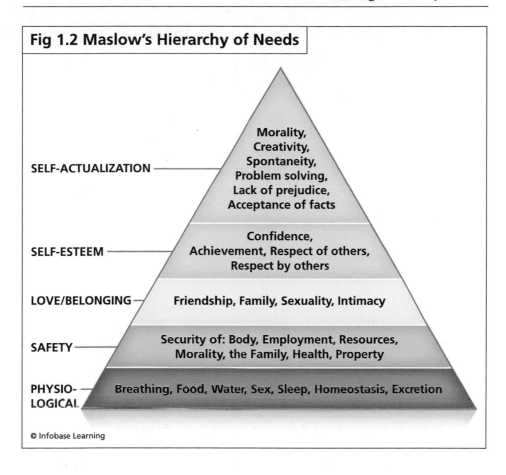

Fig 1.2 Maslow's Hierarchy of Needs

SELF-ACTUALIZATION — Morality, Creativity, Spontaneity, Problem solving, Lack of prejudice, Acceptance of facts

SELF-ESTEEM — Confidence, Achievement, Respect of others, Respect by others

LOVE/BELONGING — Friendship, Family, Sexuality, Intimacy

SAFETY — Security of: Body, Employment, Resources, Morality, the Family, Health, Property

PHYSIO-LOGICAL — Breathing, Food, Water, Sex, Sleep, Homeostasis, Excretion

© Infobase Learning

The hierarchy of needs consists of five levels of needs that parallel a developmental process. One must satisfy needs at the lower, foundational level before one can attempt to satisfy needs at the next highest level. However, achieving a particular level of need satisfaction does not guarantee that lower level needs will continue to be met. Maslow viewed needs, especially those at the lower levels of the hierarchy, as comparable to instincts that motivate behavior rather than as drives that determine behavior.

Lower levels of Maslow's hierarchy represent basic, largely physical needs, which are sometimes called **deficit needs** (or deficiency needs) because unmet needs bring a sense of deprivation. Meeting these needs assures our subsistence. Higher levels of needs—self-esteem needs and self-actualization—represent **growth needs** (or fulfillment needs) and are more psychological in nature. Meeting these needs enriches one's experience and contributes to personal growth.

Maslow's original work in the area of motivation evolved into a more comprehensive explanation of personality. Personality theorists recognized the humanistic theme that permeated Maslow's theory, particularly that part of the theory related to self-actualization. **Self-actualization** refers to the human tendency to strive towards growth and fulfillment of one's potential, and to be autonomous, self-aware, and healthy.

Carl Rogers is the best-known and most prolific advocate of a humanistic approach to understanding personality. Some of Rogers' views mirror those expressed by Maslow. Rogers, for example, believed as Maslow did that people naturally develop in healthy, positive ways and routinely seek to grow and realize their full potential. Thus, Rogers affirmed the importance of self-actualization.

The bulk of Rogers' theorizing developed from his clinical work with people and continued to evolve as he continued in his practice. Rogers believed people to be fully capable of understanding and directing their own lives. In other words, he was certain that people can and do make decisions in their own best interests. Rogers objected strenuously to theories and therapies that assumed people need some sort of external push, direction, motivation, or correction. These ideas contradicted his firm belief that people are innately good, resourceful, and trustworthy.

According to Rogers, the **actualizing tendency** prompts all living things to grow and develop in healthy ways that optimize positive outcomes and helps them to realize their full potential. As social beings, we do not accomplish these tasks in isolation from others; in fact, we need other people to help maintain an environment conducive to healthy development. As an analogy, think about a seed that needs to germinate in order to grow and produce fruit. A seed possesses all the necessary potential for a fruitful outcome. However, the seed needs good soil, adequate water, and available sunshine to get started and to keep growing. If a seed is dropped on dry pavement in the shade, its attempts to realize its full potential may be thwarted. Like seeds, people need reasonable environmental conditions to prevail.

Extrapolating from this seed analogy, we then need to ask: What do we need from our environment to assure our development unfolds in a manner that supports our reaching our full potential? According to Rogers, we need positive regard like seeds need water. **Positive regard** consists of warmth, respect, and acceptance and constitutes the lifeblood of healthy, fulfilled development. It may come to us on a conditional or an unconditional basis, and it may arise from other people or from our own self (meaning the concept one holds of oneself as an emotional, cognitive, and behavioral being).

Conditional positive regard represents a "strings attached" form of positive regard. It stems from things we *do* rather than from who we *are*. For example, a child may receive affection and approval only when (or only "on the condition" that) he or she brings home As and Bs from school. When someone must

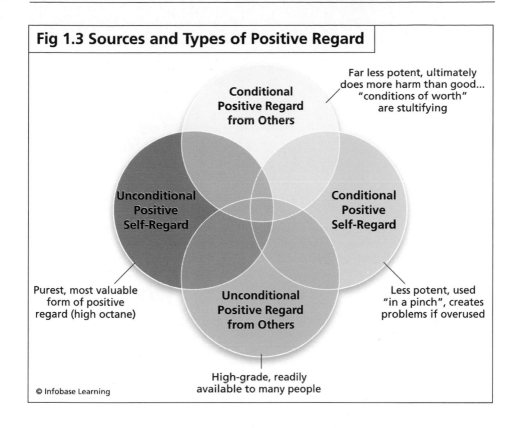

Fig 1.3 Sources and Types of Positive Regard

Conditional
Positive Regard
from Others

Far less potent, ultimately
does more harm than good...
"conditions of worth"
are stultifying

Unconditional
Positive
Self-Regard

Conditional
Positive
Self-Regard

Purest, most valuable
form of positive
regard (high octane)

Unconditional
Positive Regard
from Others

Less potent, used
"in a pinch", creates
problems if overused

© Infobase Learning

High-grade, readily
available to many people

behave in a certain way in order to secure positive regard, conditions of worth exist. **Conditions of worth** often lead to alienation from one's true feelings and isolation from one's sense of self. Conditional positive regard thwarts self-actualization because acceptance, warmth, and respect exist only under specific circumstances that very well may not align with one's own true being.

Rogers believed that optimal human growth depends upon being valued for oneself on a no-matter-what basis. **Unconditional positive regard** represents a "no strings attached" form of positive regard. Many parents demonstrate love and acceptance of their child, no matter what sorts of problems the child may cause or encounter. Many dog-owners agree that their canine companions offer them "unconditional love," which is the layperson's equivalent of unconditional positive regard.

Positive regard differs in its sources, as well. Other people can give us positive regard (conditional or unconditional) and we can give ourselves positive regard (conditional or unconditional). Overall, positive regard that comes from other people is less potent than that which we give to ourselves. Unconditional positive regard from others may not be available immediately, and conditional

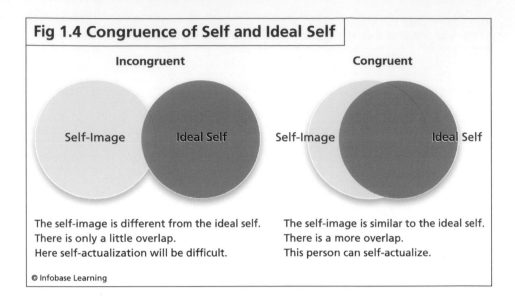

Fig 1.4 Congruence of Self and Ideal Self

Incongruent

Self-Image   Ideal Self

The self-image is different from the ideal self.
There is only a little overlap.
Here self-actualization will be difficult.

Congruent

Self-Image   Ideal Self

The self-image is similar to the ideal self.
There is a more overlap.
This person can self-actualize.

© Infobase Learning

positive regard from others may involve conditions that have little relationship to our own values.

Insufficient unconditional positive regard prompts a person to seek and settle for positive regard that is conditional. We so need positive regard that when we run low on it we will take it in whatever form we can get it. Settling for conditional positive regard creates **incongruity** between the reality of who one truly is (based on one's actual behaviors) and the person one aspires to be. This incongruence creates an unhealthy state. Preferably, our sense of self and the person we strive to be—our "ideal self"—are closely aligned.

Psychodynamic Perspective (Theories Based on Unconscious Motivation)

In the early 1900s, Sigmund Freud theorized that the most influential aspects of our personalities operate at an unconscious level. He suggested that much of our behavior results from unconscious motivations that are, by definition, out of our awareness. Like the hulking mass of an iceberg that lies beneath the surface of the water, the largest and most powerful part of personality exists below the surface of our awareness. Unconscious elements of personality reveal themselves in a variety of ways. For example, dreams and errant utterances—so-called **Freudian slips**—provide evidence that the unconscious part of our personality is alive and well.

Freud described three aspects of personality that develop within the first five or six years of life. The first of these to appear is the id. Theoretically speaking, a newborn infant is nothing but id. The **id** represents a primitive aspect of

An iceberg extends well beyond the tip that is visible from the surface of the water.
(Shutterstock)

personality, as it consists of raw, inborn, illogical, unorganized urges, wants, impulses, drives, and cravings. For the most part, these urges and drives are reducible to hostile or sexual impulses. In this context, "sexual" refers to any act that brings pleasure, not solely to sexual acts.

The id operates entirely at an unconscious level according to the pleasure principle. The pleasure principle dictates the immediate discharge of urges and

Primal, hostile urges originate in the most primitive aspect of personality—the id. *(Shutterstock)*

impulses for the purpose of relieving the tension associated with them. Thus, the id seeks immediate gratification and is not subject to the ordinary rules of polite society.

In a newborn infant, we acknowledge thrashing, screaming, and crying as the only way the newborn can express wants. These actions comprise the newborn's exclusive options because he or she possesses only a primitive, impulse-driven, demanding aspect of personality: the id. The response to the newborn's expressions is to attempt to discern what is wanted and provide it (quickly!). Of course, we would not tolerate such behavior in an older child or a grownup. Fortunately, we generally do not have to tolerate such antics, as another aspect of personality—the ego—begins to develop within the first several months of life.

The **ego** represents a mostly unconscious, rational counterpart to the irrational and demanding id. The ego responds to the demands of the id, but does so by employing the **reality principle**. According to this principle, the ego subdues the id and channels its energy to find realistic, safe, and socially acceptable ways to satisfy the id's desires.

The final aspect of personality develops in early childhood, typically between about 4 and 6 years of age. This structure, the **superego**, operates primarily on an unconscious level and embodies society's morals, as taught by significant others—primarily parents and teachers. One part of the superego, the **ego-ideal**, motivates us to behave in morally appropriate ways. The second part, the **conscience**, generates guilt when we behave in morally inappropriate ways.

Like the id, the superego is a demanding and unrealistic taskmaster. It impels virtuous behavior and pushes us to become perfect—rather a tall order. Under ordinary circumstances, there is a dynamic tension among the different aspects of personality. **Libido** is the psychic energy that drives all of these different aspects. The ego functions as the executive of personality, mediating disputes among the constituents, ever mindful of the constraints imposed by reality.

Freud also explained development as a progression through a series of **psychosexual stages**—oral, anal, phallic, latency, and genital. Within each stage except latency, an individual derives pleasure primarily through a specific zone of the body—the **erogenous zone**. Each stage of development also involves a crucial conflict that must be resolved as completely as possible so that the individual can move on to the next stage. Once again, libido fuels conflict resolution, and the individual must invest psychic energy to resolve the conflict.

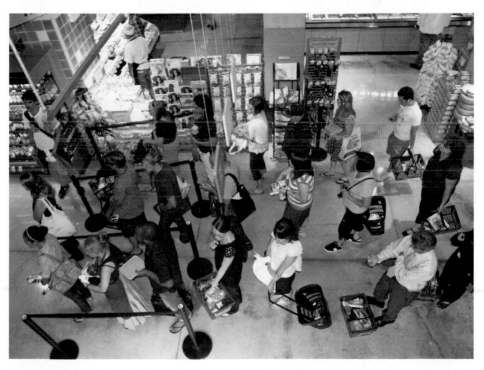

The ego helps us to handle the reality of delaying gratification. *(David Shankbone. Wikipedia)*

The superego maintains our moral compass, which impels us to return a found wallet to its rightful owner. *(Wikipedia)*

Imperfect conflict resolution results in fixations that continue to consume energy. **Fixations** represent leftover conflicts or portions thereof that are thematically linked to the developmental stage in which they first appeared. For example, a person who fails to resolve the crucial conflict of the oral stage (weaning), continues to experience oral issues. The oral fixation would be evident even much later in that person's life, in the form of excessive oral activities—smoking, gum chewing, or talking, for example.

As described above, the three aspects of personality have different agendas or priorities, all of which require libido to fuel them. And fuel is limited. Thus, the conflicts between or among the id, ego, and superego can be understood as power struggles. Each aspect wants more libido directed toward satisfying its demands. The most demanding parts of personality are those that function outside the realm of reality—that is, the id and the superego. For many people, these two aspects generate much unconscious turmoil, bits and pieces of which become apparent as elements of dreams or as symptoms.

The ego—as the more pragmatic, reality bound entity—must remain ready to intervene and resolve conflicts that occur. Within the psychodynamic framework, anxiety serves to warn the ego that conflicts are about to erupt. Thus, anxiety is a symptom of unconscious havoc that threatens to overthrow the ego's rational, orderly control. The kind of anxiety one experiences relates to the nature of conflict, with **neurotic anxiety** being the most common form.

The ego uses **defense mechanisms** to confront anxiety. Like most other elements of Freud's theory, most defenses operate at an unconscious level. In addition, all defenses consume psychic energy, although some are more efficient (i.e., use less energy and work better) than others. Defenses reduce anxiety by masking its source. Thus, all defenses involve a distortion of reality. But solutions that distort reality work rather well in this system because neither the id nor the superego operates as a reality-bound entity.

For many years, Freud's theory of personality dominated the theory and practice of clinical psychology. There is little scientific evidence to support the basic premises of Freud's theory (and it, like other aspects of his work, continues to generate controversy), but it does offer an explanation for otherwise inexplicable, heinous acts (e.g., violence and sexual aggression) more completely than many other theories. Indeed, it is quite difficult to fathom how humanists such as Maslow or Rogers would explain such vile actions.

Historically, Freud's views spawned a number of other personality theories, some comprising derivatives of his work and others that developed directly from other theorists' opposition to Freud's notions about personality. For

Fig 1.5 Types and Causes of Anxiety

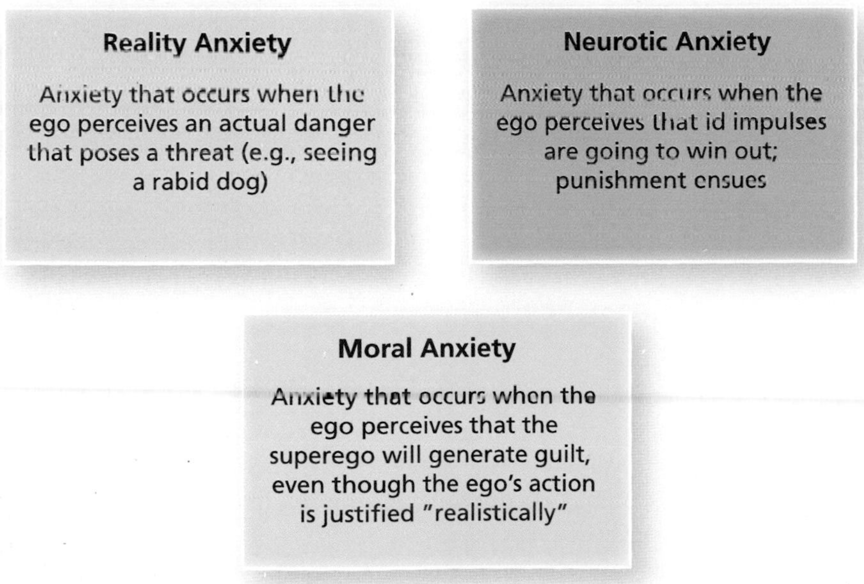

Reality Anxiety

Anxiety that occurs when the ego perceives an actual danger that poses a threat (e.g., seeing a rabid dog)

Neurotic Anxiety

Anxiety that occurs when the ego perceives that id impulses are going to win out; punishment ensues

Moral Anxiety

Anxiety that occurs when the ego perceives that the superego will generate guilt, even though the ego's action is justified "realistically"

© Infobase Learning

Sample of Ego Defense Mechanisms

Repression is the unconscious exclusion of anxiety-provoking thoughts and memories from our awareness. Many people employ this mechanism rather successfully to keep anxieties at bay. The defense mechanism of *suppression* operates in a similar fashion, but on a conscious level.

Denial represents a simplistic, primitive defense against anxiety. This defense consists of blatant ignorance of the existence of threatening material. Denial is similar to repression but operates on a more conscious level. It amounts to a massive distortion of reality and consumes a great deal of psychic energy to perpetuate the charade.

Reaction formation begins with a mostly unconscious denial of unacceptable impulses followed by a mostly conscious substitution of the opposite urge with behavioral correlates. For example, an individual may deny hostile urges towards a relative or an in-law and treat that person with great deference and kindness.

Displacement occurs when tension stemming from anxiety is discharged onto a safer and available target. The silly idea that one should punch a pillow when angry derives from a misunderstanding of this mechanism. Displacement operates only on an unconscious level.

Projection results from a misattribution of an unacceptable impulse in oneself to another party. A hallmark of paranoid processing, this defense mechanism preserves ego integrity by grossly distorting reality.

In *regression*, the individual avoids conflict by retreating to an earlier stage of development, when such threats and attendant anxiety did not exist. Thus, a 7-year-old continent child under stress may regress to an earlier stage of development, as might become evident by renewed bedwetting.

In *identification*, the individual adopts the role and attitudes of a more powerful and therefore threatening individual. For example, some prisoners of war who are under tremendous threat of harm become minions of their captors.

Sublimation involves channeling unacceptable urges and impulses into socially acceptable, even socially admirable, activities. For example, an individual with hostile urges to dismember others may redirect those impulses and become a surgeon.

example, behaviorists rejected outright the idea that hidden, inner workings of our minds were responsible for our behaviors. Instead, they proposed exactly the opposite by suggesting that purely external (environmental) events served to establish and shape those behaviors.

Other psychodynamic theorists include Carl Jung and Alfred Adler. Originally, both were disciples of Freud who gradually moved away from Freud's notions to develop their own theories of personality. Jung deemphasized the sexual aspects of Freud's theory and focused on events he believed took place during middle age. He suggested middle age as the time when we must confront our unconscious and, ultimately, integrate the sometimes unseemly aspects contained therein with our conscious understanding of our identity—a process termed **individuation**.

Jung's theory is broad and complicated, with contributions from history, mythology, and religion. The theory promotes the importance of the unconscious, including dreams. Jung held that dreams represented more than just a tricky way for the unconscious to have its way with our psyche. He believed that our dreams contained helpful messages about the sometimes dark nature of our unconscious—our **shadow**. Allowing expression of unconscious elements helps us to know and then integrate these aspects of our personality with conscious aspects. Jung conceptualized our search for life's meaning as a force that pulls us towards fulfillment and the realization of our potential—clearly, a humanistic thread runs through his theory.

Alfred Adler was another of Freud's contemporaries and an early contributor to the development of the psychodynamic perspective. After several years of collaboration, Freud and Adler parted company. Adler differed with Freud on a great many points, including the source of human motivation. Adler believed that social relatedness, rather than sexual impulses, motivated behavior. Although he agreed that early childhood was a crucial time in development, he asserted that its importance derived from the opportunities it created for the child—that is, opportunities that allowed the child to begin to understand how the social world works. It was during this time, he argued, that people begin to form an approach to life.

Adler valued the conscious realm and believed that people make purposeful choices, based on their perceptions and interpretations of early events in their lives. According to Adler, by the time an individual reaches about 6 years of age, he or she develops a **life goal** that is consistent with an idealized view of the self as perfect and complete. This life goal provides motivation and inspires us to overcome **feelings of inferiority**. **Striving for superiority** is a natural quest and reflects a general tendency to reach one's personal best rather than to obliterate the competition.

CONCLUSION

Personality forms the framework through which we view, interpret, and interact with the environment and events that take place within it. The characteristics a person possesses provide him or her with a predictable behavioral repertoire. A variety of theories have been advanced to explain how one's personality is established and, possibly, shaped over the course of one's lifetime or through specific experiences. Some theorists assert that personality can be understood only through the actions demonstrated by an individual while other theorists posit that actions frequently belie one's true motives, which are so primitive and socially unacceptable that they are unknown even to the actor. Social influences are seen as central by some personality theorists who hold that much of our behavior can be attributed to our living as social beings and learning through observing the actions of other people. Still other theorists value human nature and the potential it holds for helping us to develop in healthy, productive ways and to achieve all that is humanly possible for each individual

Each perspective discussed in this chapter approaches the study of personality differently, and each has attendant advantages and disadvantages. Within each broad perspective, specific theories of personality continue to evolve. Some recent approaches to understanding personality do not derive directly from any one perspective. For example, Martin Seligman reconceptualized human nature, launching a movement that emphasizes positive aspects of human existence, reflective of a humanistic perspective, whereas his concept of learned optimism connotes a behavioral slant.

For the most part, the perspectives on personality discussed in this chapter explain generically how personality develops and can be applied to normal personality development. As described in the next chapter, the theories also can help explain what has gone wrong when behavioral aberrations occur.

Further Reading

Bandura, A. "Social Cognitive Theory: An Agentic Perspective." *Annual Review of Psychology* 52 (2001): 1–52.

Friedman, H.S., and M.W. Schustrack. *Readings in Personality: Classic Theorists and Modern Research*. Boston: Allyn & Bacon, 2001.

Maslow, A.H. "Some Basic Propositions of a Growth and Self-actualization Psychology." In *Toward a Psychology of Being* (pp. 189–214). New York: Von Nostrund, 1962. Available at http://psychclassics.yorku.ca/Maslow/motivation.htm.

Mitchell, S.A., and M.J. Black. *Freud and Beyond: A History of Modern Psychoanalytic Thought*. New York: Basic Books, 1995.

Mosak, H.H., and M.P. Maniacci. *Primer of Adlerian Psychology*. New York: Brunner/Routledge, 1999.

Roberts, B.W., and W.F. DelVecchio. "The Rank-order Consistency of Personality Traits from Childhood to Old Age: A Quantitative Review of Longitudinal Studies." *Psychological Bulletin* 126 (2000): 3–25.

Rogers, C.R. *A Way of Being*. Boston: Houghton-Mifflin, 1980.

Schultz, D., and S.E. Schultz. *Theories of Personality*. 8th ed. Pacific Grove, Calif.: Brooks/Cole, 2005.

CHAPTER 2

UNDERSTANDING ABNORMAL BEHAVIOR

Some behavior that we witness daily can be quite odd, and this raises several important questions. Where does normal behavior end and abnormal behavior begin? Under what, if any conditions are ordinary behaviors regarded as abnormal? When does peculiar behavior become outright bizarre? In this chapter, we respond to these questions by summarizing methods employed to define abnormal behavior, reviewing the ways in which history recounts abnormal behavior, and considering how four major theoretical perspectives frame abnormal behavior.

DEFINING ABNORMAL BEHAVIOR

Psychologists utilize several approaches to determine whether a behavior is abnormal. Specifically, we are likely to consider the extent to which a given behavior (a) deviates from average or typical behavior, (b) deviates from ideal behavior, (c) creates subjective distress in the individual who demonstrates the behavior, or (d) indicates an inability to function effectively in society. Each of these considerations comprises a criterion that, if met, signals the existence of a behavioral anomaly.

Deviation from Average Behavior

Many terms describe normal behavior; among those we use are ordinary, typical, common, and usual. Equivalent terms for abnormal behavior include extraordinary, atypical, uncommon, and unusual. But in psychology, the term "normal" often conveys statistical meaning as well. Qualities of interest within psychology that follow a **normal distribution** resemble a bell shaped curve when the scores representing the construct are plotted against their frequency of occurrence. Normal refers to the nature (essentially, the shape) of the curve. The highest point of such a curve indicates the most frequently obtained score. In fact, the height of the curve above any specific score indicates the frequency with which the score occurred in the population that produced the scores.

To illustrate the foregoing point, consider the construct of intelligence. Psychologists believe that intelligence is normally distributed within the population. This means that most people taking intelligence tests score at or near the middle of the distribution of all possible scores. The middle of a normal distribution represents the average (or mean) score—in this case, an IQ value of 100. Some people's scores are somewhat above average; some are somewhat below average. Rarely do people score far above average or far below average.

Truly extreme IQ values occur so infrequently that they are considered abnormal because they represent clear deviations from the average. In some cases, designating extreme IQ values as abnormal may substantiate a need for subsequent beneficial actions. For example, below average intelligence is one criterion that must be met to justify a diagnosis of mental retardation (see Chapter 4 for more detailed information on this) and prompt educational approaches that differ significantly from educational norms. Above average intelligence can also create a need for educational modifications—for example, placement in a "gifted" program. Other psychological attributes besides intelligence may follow a normal distribution as well. For example, it is easy to envision personality traits such as openness (or conscientiousness, extroversion, agreeableness, neuroticism) as normally distributed within the general population. If so, then we expect most people to be moderately open to new experiences, some would be somewhat more open, and some would be somewhat less open. Few people would deviate greatly from average and demonstrate extreme openness or extreme resistance to novel ideas and experiences.

Considering whether behavior deviates from typical (i.e., average) behavior generally boils down to a statistical method of judging which behaviors qualify as normal or abnormal. However, this approach flags as abnormal all exceptional behaviors, some of which do not cause consternation and do not require intervention. Examples of this situation would include excessive conscientiousness or excessive agreeableness—clearly exceptional (and perhaps desirable) behaviors that are statistically rare.

Deviation from Ideal Behavior
Another way to view behavior and judge its normalcy involves an evaluation of how well an individual's actions align with established ideals for that behavior.

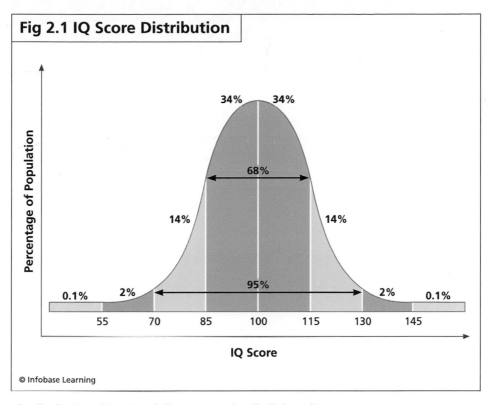

Fig 2.1 IQ Score Distribution

Percentage of Population (y-axis)

34%   34%

68%

14%   14%

95%

0.1%   2%   2%   0.1%

55   70   85   100   115   130   145

IQ Score

© Infobase Learning

The distribution of IQ values follows a normal or "bell-shaped" curve.

Often, these ideals embody the prevailing values of society. Ideal behaviors also depend somewhat on the specific context(s) within which they occur.

For example, classroom contexts within the United States generally encourage behaviors that promote optimal learning for all students. In this context, ideal behaviors consist of those actions that reflect cooperation and respect for others (e.g., taking turns, speaking when called upon, listening to others as they speak). On the other hand, behaviors that interfere with this goal represent deviations from ideal behaviors (e.g., interrupting others or calling out during a lesson, engaging in tasks unrelated to the educational activity that is underway). Of course, simply calling out in class is not abnormal in and of itself. Isolated instances of aberrant behavior may occur without causing concern. In addition, behavior that is suspicious for abnormality must be evaluated in context.

Arguably, viewing and evaluating normal and abnormal behavior within a context represents an improvement over the purely statistical method of assessing deviance from average, partly because, when viewed in context, exceptional behaviors that reflect ideal behaviors are not generally labeled abnormal. However, the approach depends on a clear understanding of accepted standards of behavior that constitute ideals. In multicultural societies such as the United States, a singular standard for any one behavior is extremely difficult (and maybe impossible) to establish.

Another problem with this method of evaluating abnormality relates to the subjectivity of the individual doing the evaluating. Almost invariably, this person will exercise his or her own judgment (including any biases that may exist) about a given action even before attempting to discern whether it deviates from ideal behavior. For example, if a student calls out a relevant question during a lesson, one teacher may consider that behavior an interruption whereas another teacher may view the same behavior as positive engagement or participation.

Sense of Personal Distress

Our discussion thus far has focused on the use of an external standard (population average or ideal behavior) to discriminate between normal and abnormal behavior. Another approach involves the use of an internal indicator. **Subjective distress** refers to the perceived level of stress, dissatisfaction, despair, tension, confusion, fear, and anxiety an individual experiences. Although life has its ups and downs, we generally expect people to muster sufficient fortitude to cope with trying situations and to resolve them without falling apart, something that is more likely to occur with individuals with high levels of subjective distress. Thus, higher subjective distress levels qualify as abnormal.

The concept of subjective distress rests on the premise that what matters most is how individuals perceive their experiences, rather than the actual nature of those experiences. A certain experience can send one person into a tailspin whereas another person faced with the same situation may appear unflappable and simply take it in stride. In other words, the degree of distress experienced by each individual differs even though the problem may be the same for both people.

Individuals experiencing high levels of subjective distress frequently report their distress to other people, including family members and friends. Subjective distress often feels wrong to the sufferer and sometimes also prompts him or her to seek assistance from a therapist or counselor. In this respect, subjective distress as an indicator of abnormal behavior differs markedly from the deviance models described previously. A person whose behavior deviates from average behavior or from an ideal behavior may or may not experience discomfort because of that deviation. In contrast, a person whose behavior causes him or her subjective distress experiences discomfort that sometimes manifests itself in rather obvious symptoms (e.g., insomnia, gastrointestinal upset, changes in weight).

Inability to Function Effectively

Another way to distinguish abnormal behavior from normal behavior derives from what society expects from its competent members. Fully functioning members of society attend to their daily living needs (e.g., bathing), manage

Subjective Units of Disturbance Scale

In the late 1960s, Joseph Wolpe developed a now widely used scale to assess current levels of discomfort or psychological pain. Called the Subjective Units of Disturbance Scale (or SUDS), this self-report scale has a 0 to 10 range of responses, where 0 reflects no discomfort and 10 reflects the worst discomfort the test taker can imagine. It provides a benchmark by which to evaluate treatment progress.

Rating	Associated Feelings and Self Descriptions
0	Serene and peaceful; reports no bad feelings of any kind
1	Basically good; reports feeling good with perhaps distant awareness of mildly unpleasant feeling
2	Slightly disgruntled; reports feeling pretty good with awareness of unpleasant feelings that can be brought to the surface with effort
3	Mildly worried, disgruntled, or unhappy; reports being bothered
4	Somewhat upset; reports unpleasant thoughts or feelings that cannot be ignored easily
5	Moderately upset and uncomfortable; reports feeling able still to manage unpleasant feelings
6	Quite upset, unhappy, uncomfortable; reports belief that something needs to be done to change the way he or she feels
7	Very upset; reports feeling on edge and that his or her ability to manage unpleasant feelings is stretched to capacity
8	Extremely upset; reports feeling isolated and wonders how long he or she can remain in control
9	Desperation and fear, coupled with very bad feelings; reports unbearable disturbance and feeling that loss of control is imminent
10	Overwhelmed and not in control; reports feelings of unbearable and unending discomfort that are beyond his or her control and beyond help offered by others

financial affairs (e.g., paying bills), participate in leisure activities (e.g., posting tweets to Twitter), manage household tasks (e.g., taking out the trash), and either hold jobs, go to school, or care for others (e.g., children). Individuals who cannot or do not fulfill these nominal expectations demonstrate abnormal behavior.

Individuals incapable of fending for themselves require assistance. Yet many people who fail to meet ordinary societal expectations for adequate functioning are not able to recognize their inability to do so. Some insist that they *do* meet these expectations, despite obvious evidence to the contrary. For example, a person with moderate Alzheimer's disease (a progressive form of dementia that primarily affects older adults) may argue that he or she took a shower yesterday when, in fact, he or she has not bathed in more than a week. Notably, such a person very likely believes what he or she said is accurate and is not purposefully telling a lie. Hoarders, people suffering from bulimia, and others with behavioral disorders have a similar inability to recognize that a problem exists.

Most individuals who demonstrate hoarding behaviors do not recognize the behavior as problematic. The sheer number of animals housed in small spaces quickly creates squalid and unhealthy conditions for the animals as well as for any humans who live in the same space, but an animal hoarder will often insist that all is well and that the arrangement is mutually beneficial. *(Wikipedia)*

In some cases, family members may provide needed assistance for individuals whose functioning is not effective. When family solutions are not viable, individuals who are grossly disabled in terms of life skills often require public assistance. State and federal agencies in the United States are obligated protect all members of the public, and arranging care for those who cannot care for themselves constitutes a related obligation.

In the most extreme cases, commitment to a psychiatric treatment facility may occur. All states have laws that permit holding certain individuals against their will in general hospitals or psychiatric centers. Most **involuntary commitment** procedures require signatures from more than one licensed mental health practitioner (e.g., two physicians or a physician and a psychologist) and specify that a person so detained can be held only for a limited period of time—often 72 hours. After that, a person may (or may choose not to) agree to receive treatment that entails voluntary admission or outpatient treatment.

Although defining abnormal behavior is important, it is equally important to understand it. Perhaps no one can communicate better the nature and impact of a mental disorder than someone with firsthand experience. Several individuals have written compelling books that detail their struggles with a variety of mental disorders. In addition, parents, partners, and children (and sometimes biographers) of individuals with psychological disorders offer poignant insights about the challenges posed by mental disorders.

Some Biographical and Autobiographical Accounts of Mental Disorders

Beers, C. *A Mind That Found Itself: An Autobiography.* Garden City, New York: Doubleday, 1907. (schizophrenia)

Garson, S. "The Sound and the Fury of Mania." *Newsweek* 109 (April 13, 1987): 10. (mood disorder)

Kaysen, S. *Girl Interrupted.* New York: Turtle Bay Books, 1993. (personality disorder)

Nasar, S. *A Beautiful Mind: A Biography of John Forbes Nash, Jr.* New York: Simon & Schuster, 1998. (schizophrenia)

Styron, W. *Darkness Visible: A Memoir of Madness.* New York: Vintage Books, 1990. (depression)

Volkmar, F.R. and D.J. Cohen. "The Experience of Infantile Autism: A First-person Account by Tony W." *Journal of Autism and Developmental Disorders* 15 (1985): 47–54. (developmental disorder)

Most biographical and autobiographical accounts comprise success stories as the authors delineate the trials of and ultimate triumphs over serious mental health conditions. These accounts illuminate the nature of a particular disorder, as experienced by a specific individual. As such, they do not represent each and every experience of each and every other individual with the same disorder. Nevertheless, firsthand accounts of life with a mental disorder provide unique vantage points that help us to appreciate the basic nature of certain disorders.

In Chapter 1 we reviewed the major strategies used by psychologists to understand personality and its associated ordinary behavior. In this chapter our primary goal is to describe approaches used to understand abnormal behavior. Part of this description must include a historical overview of abnormal behaviors and how they have been perceived.

HISTORICAL VIEWS OF ABNORMAL BEHAVIOR

Human behavior and its varied forms have existed for as long as human beings themselves. According to standards in place, some behaviors were viewed as aberrant even centuries ago. So how did people from long ago explain odd or aberrant behavior that did not conform to the standards of the time?

Abnormal Behavior in Ancient Times

If you think it difficult to comprehend unusual, peculiar, or outright bizarre behavior now, just imagine the challenge faced by ancient peoples who did not have the benefit of logic and true scientific reasoning to explain such things. For them, behaviors (as well as many other phenomena) were veiled in mystery. Ready explanations tended to invoke supernatural or spiritual forces such as celestial movements, the wrath of a supreme being, or the work of evil spirits.

When someone was thought to be possessed by evil spirits, ancient practices involved attempts to rid the afflicted person of those spirits. Such efforts included benign attempts to coax the spirit out of its habitat through prayer or special potions that the possessed person was given to drink. More brutal efforts included a variety of techniques that made an afflicted person's body a less comfortable place for the spirit to reside. For example, an individual might be held under water, deprived of food, or subjected to physical torture such as flogging or trephining.

Trephining was one of the most extreme practices employed by ancient peoples to free an individual from evil spirits. The practice involved drilling a hole (usually about an inch in diameter) into the skull of a living person. Some psychologists believe that the intent was to create a passage through which evil spirits could exit the body of the possessed person. Other psychologists suggest that the practice may have been used to treat physical rather than behavioral problems, and specifically, head injuries such as those that created blood clots, bone splinters, or bone fragments.

Physiology and Abnormal Behavior

Ancient Greek societies also explained mental disturbances as supernatural and spiritual phenomena. Later, these societies developed a more naturalistic approach to understanding abnormal behavior. The Greek physician

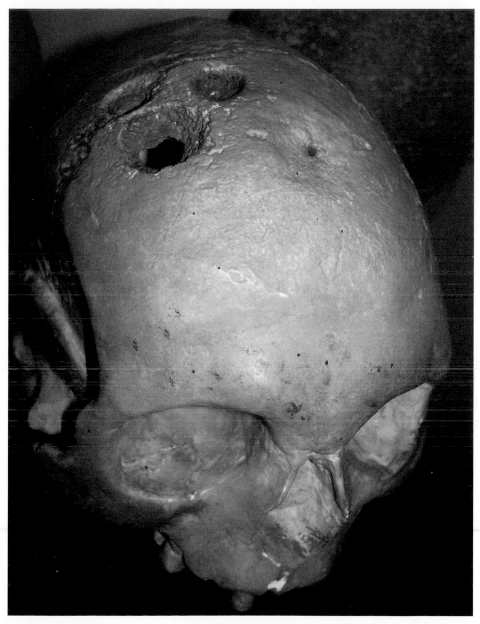

Trephined skull. *(Wikipedia. Courtesy of High Contrast)*

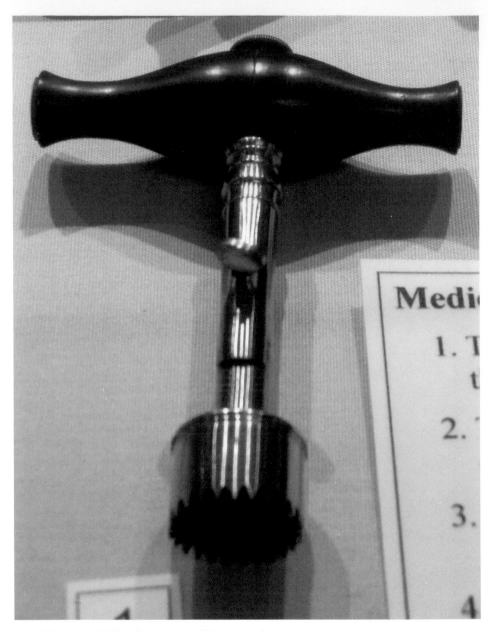

Trephining tool. *(Wikipedia. Courtesy of Green Lane)*

Hippocrates, who lived from about 460 years B.C. to about 360 years B.C., abandoned supernatural explanations for all illnesses, including mental illness. Instead, he used an **empirical approach** to explain them—one that included observing and describing instances of mental illness, including epilepsy and phobias.

Hippocrates also developed a biologically based **explanation** for abnormal behavior. He theorized that mental disorders developed primarily from internal processes, although he allowed that external factors might also influence the course of these disorders. Hippocrates suggested that personality (temperament) disorders developed as a result of imbalances among the body's four vital fluids or **humors**: blood, black bile, yellow bile, and phlegm. Excess levels of a specific humor produced a specific personality type with clearly identifiable characteristics.

Although his temperament theory involving bodily fluids proved incorrect, Hippocrates established an important new way of thinking about physical and mental illnesses—one that incorporated physiology and biology. Many

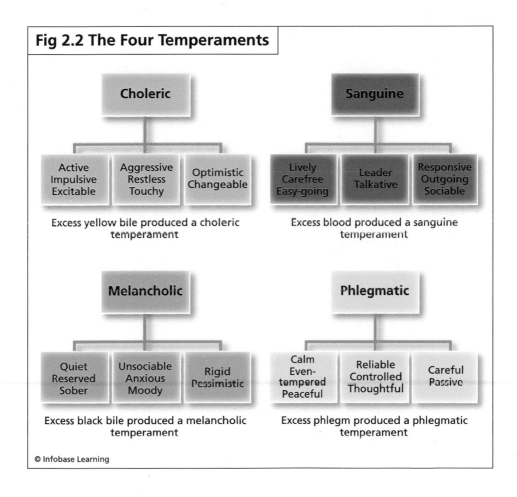

Fig 2.2 The Four Temperaments

Choleric

| Active Impulsive Excitable | Aggressive Restless Touchy | Optimistic Changeable |

Excess yellow bile produced a choleric temperament

Sanguine

| Lively Carefree Easy-going | Leader Talkative | Responsive Outgoing Sociable |

Excess blood produced a sanguine temperament

Melancholic

| Quiet Reserved Sober | Unsociable Anxious Moody | Rigid Pessimistic |

Excess black bile produced a melancholic temperament

Phlegmatic

| Calm Even-tempered Peaceful | Reliable Controlled Thoughtful | Careful Passive |

Excess phlegm produced a phlegmatic temperament

centuries later, modern perspectives on abnormal behavior include constitutionally based explanations that reflect his way of thinking. In addition, by advocating humane, noninvasive treatments such as rest, exercise, and a bland diet, Hippocrates laid the foundation for compassionate care of individuals with mental disorders.

The Influence of Religion

The rise of the Roman Empire preserved the basic tenets put forth by the Greeks concerning mental health. Science continued to gain ground until Rome fell in the 5th century, after a succession of invasions by tribes from northern Europe. Thereafter, scientific pursuits (along with most other scholarly and artistic pursuits) came to a rather abrupt end.

During the Middle Ages, there was a resurgence of interest in learning, and scientific ideas and findings were once again elevated. However, scientific theories of the time—including those used to understand mental illness—emerged in an environment characterized by strong religious beliefs. And just as their ancestors had once believed in the power of evil spirits to cause abnormal behavior, the people of the Middle Ages often viewed abnormal behavior as the work of the devil. As you might expect, efforts to cast out the devil again ranged from benign to barbarous.

Later, during the Renaissance era, abnormal behavior continued to be viewed in part as the work of the devil. However, another mysterious evil—witchcraft—was thought to explain outlandish behavior equally well. The church fully endorsed witch hunts to root out and punish practitioners of witchcraft. Hysteria and paranoia ran high, and as people regarded the eradication of witches as both a civic and a religious duty, citizens and congregants often turned on each other.

The extent to which individuals with mental disorders were swept up and punished as witches is not known with any certainty. The climate of the times established a low threshold of tolerance that invoked a better-safe-than-sorry rule. Thus, mental illness and its associated aberrant behaviors were often more than likely to be interpreted and reported as evidence of witchcraft.

But this was not always the case. There were times when psychological disturbances continued to be understood as illnesses, and local governments sometimes absorbed responsibility for those who were mentally ill, seeing to it that their basic needs were met. The quality of care was highly variable and emphasized custodial aspects of care that could be quite harsh (e.g., imprisonment and bondage). Although some individuals with mental illnesses received community-based care, many of those afflicted were relegated to general hospitals or mental hospitals known as **asylums**. This practice flourished during the 1700s and was only marginally better than the practices of earlier times. Many institutionalized patients, restrained by chains or in cages, were put on display, as entertainment for the general public. In some instances, tickets were sold to curious would-be spectators.

Moral Therapy Gains Support

Reform efforts eventually emerged with the dawn of the 19th century. The first of these were spearheaded by Jean-Baptiste Pussin and Phillipe Pinel in France and William Tuke in northern England.

Pussin served as superintendent of an "incurables" ward at a large hospital in Paris. He had no special training or experience in mental illness, but upon his appointment, he introduced major changes in how patients were to be treated. For example, he forbade beating patients and insisted upon unchaining a group of patients with apparently severe and intractable disorders. To the surprise of the staff, more humane treatment produced more manageable patients. Pinel and Tuke carried Pussin's ideas further, replacing inhumane treatments with far more therapeutic ones. Among the methods they recommended were talking to patients and providing quiet, supportive settings. Despite considerable resistance, these new tactics showed merit and became much more widely used.

Proponents of **moral therapy,** as the new techniques were known, regarded persons with mental disturbances as normal persons who shouldered unusually heavy and burdensome problems. Restoration depended upon providing a proper situation (e.g., safe, pleasant, quiet environment) in which their problems could be addressed (e.g., through conversation and some gainful employment).

In the United States, it was Benjamin Rush who first drew attention to the matter of mental illness. During the latter 1700s and early 1800s, Rush created the first academic course in psychiatry and drew medicine and mental illness closer together. Although some of his ideas about treatments appear uninformed by today's standards, Rush's intentions were noble and centered upon alleviating distress.

Shortly after Rush's passing, Dorothea Dix took up the cause of individuals who were both poor and mentally ill. She worked tirelessly during the mid-1800s as an advocate for government involvement to advance the humane treatment of indigent individuals with mental disorders. Her efforts paved the way for the establishment of mental asylums (public mental hospitals) in the United States.

In the years to come, state governments constructed many facilities to provide treatment for destitute mentally ill citizens. Most of these institutions comprised sprawling campuses, built on the outskirts of towns or cities where land was available and reasonably priced. The pastoral settings provided peaceful retreats. Unfortunately, public perceptions of state mental hospitals tended

Dorothea Dix (1802–1887), a schoolteacher from Boston, advocated for humane treatment of individuals with mental disorders. *(Library of Congress)*

toward fear and uncertainty, in part because the patients were cordoned off from mainstream society. Furthermore, the number of institutions built outstripped the number of workers available to deliver services. Many facilities provided little more than shelter to their residents.

The Medical Model and Psychogenic Explanations

At about the same time that state-run institutions were proliferating, moral therapy fell from favor as medical professionals began to regard mental disorders as illnesses that resulted from biological abnormalities and diseases. They argued that a **medical model** could best explain and treat psychological disorders. The ideas advanced by Pinel and Tuke, which put a premium on offering patients a therapeutic environment, were largely pushed aside, and hospital staff moved toward biologically based theories and treatments.

During the latter part of the 19th century, a number of new theories were advanced to explain abnormal behavior and offer treatment alternatives. Notably, Emil Kraepelin proposed that brain pathology played a central role in mental disturbances. Kraepelin also devised a classification for mental disorders similar to that used to classify physical disorders. These two developments provided tremendous support for the expansion of the medical model, which seemed to hold considerable promise as far as the treatment of conditions previously deemed intractable.

Alternative explanations for psychological disorders also developed during this time period. In contrast to the prevailing **somatogenic** belief that pathological (essentially diseased) conditions of body structures accounted for mental illness, advocates of a **psychogenic** theory held that emotional or psychological pressures gave rise to mental disturbances. The heightened suggestibility of patients undergoing hypnosis offered supportive evidence for the psychogenic theory.

The initial inroads regarding hypnosis were made by three physicians: Mesmer, Liébeault, and Bernheim. Soon thereafter, came Freud's early therapeutic efforts, which made plentiful use of hypnotic techniques. Near the turn of the 20th century, Freud's work, along with that of his colleague Josef Breuer, served to strengthen the idea that the human mind was accessible to psychological treatment in the form of a "talking cure."

CONTEMPORARY VIEWS OF ABNORMAL BEHAVIOR

Modern views of abnormal behavior align with the broad theoretical perspectives on personality described in Chapter 1. Specific theorists associated with each of these perspectives have utilized broad premises on which these theories are based to explain how abnormal behavior develops and, in some cases, the purpose it serves. Initially, a number of individual theorists relied upon their experiences conducting therapy to develop and refine their ideas about abnormal behavior. Thus, the broad theoretical perspectives often gave rise to a number of more specific theories as practitioners refined and extended the basic principles of a given theoretical orientation.

Trait Theorists' View of Abnormal Behavior

Trait theorists endorse the view that we are born with physical and psychological traits. Thus, what we observe as another's personality is a composite of constitutionally based or biological influences that are primarily genetic in origin. Trait theorists also acknowledge that the environment can influence the expression of psychological traits, just as it can influence physical traits.

According to trait theorists, specific traits that exist within individuals may act in isolation or in combination with other traits to produce behaviors, including abnormal behaviors. For example, an individual who is *excitable, flamboyant, creative,* and *energetic* may demonstrate behavior that appears normal under some circumstances and abnormal—perhaps unruly or manic—under others. (See Chapter 4 for more information about mood disorders.)

Learning Perspectives on Abnormal Behavior

Learning theorists posit that behavior (normal and abnormal) develops from experience. Specifically, behavior is shaped by repeated exposure to patterns of rewards and punishments associated with or following specific actions. Many learning theorists also recognize that people **generalize** learned behaviors, meaning that they use a learned response in similar—but not necessarily identical—situations.

For example, a child who receives a reward for saying "thank you" to his mother when she offers a cookie will say "thank you" to any adult who offers a treat. This example illustrates two forms of generalization. The child first generalizes from *mother* to *any adult* and then generalizes from *cookie* to *treat*. Generalization helps to explain the vast array of complex human behaviors not specifically subject to a system of reinforcements (rewards) or punishments. Many abnormal behaviors, especially highly deviant ones (e.g., killing a person and dismembering the corpse), are not established simply by patterns of rewards and punishments.

Observational learning is a modified version of strict (radical) behavior theory and can also account for the acquisition of normal or abnormal behaviors. As noted in Chapter 1, any behavior that is merely observed may be imitated. If the observer also witnesses desirable outcomes associated with the observed behavior, the tendency to imitate the behavior will be strengthened. Some abnormal behaviors may develop in just this way, through direct observation or vicarious experiences.

Humanistic Perspectives on Abnormal Behavior
The humanistic perspective centers on the worth of human beings as individuals. This perspective incorporates human values, interests, and welfare. Theorists who support a humanistic approach to personality believe that people naturally develop in ways that help them reach and fulfill their potential. It may seem hard to fathom that such an optimistic perspective can account for behavioral irregularities!

This anomaly is easier to grasp with an understanding that the humanistic perspective is in some ways an idealized overview of behavior. In other words, this perspective uses a generally positive framework to delineate what ordinarily happens to people as they grow and develop. But theorists within this framework also understand that ordinary life includes roadblocks. In rare cases, these roadblocks may occur in close succession to one another, effectively halting healthy development. And it is in such circumstances that abnormal behavior can emerge.

As explained by Carl Rogers, an individual who experiences a shortfall in unconditional positive regard (that is, whose worth is conditional and valued only if certain behaviors are demonstrated or specific goals are reached) will behave in ways that are atypical and therefore untrue to the actual self in an effort to secure even a watered down version of positive regard (e.g., conditional positive regard from other people). But behavior that is inconsistent with one's identity is disingenuous as well as abnormal. In the long run, it is not sustainable.

The humanistic perspective closely reflects the idea that the most dependable index of abnormal behavior is subjective distress. We experience distress when we perceive that we have stopped moving toward the ultimate humanistic goal of self-actualization (the tendency to strive toward growth and fulfillment of one's potential as an autonomous being). This feels wrong and we

Case Study: Man on the Street

While walking down the street one weekday afternoon around 3:00 p.m., you notice a man walking toward you. The man appears to be in his mid-30s, trim, and disheveled. His hair is long and uncombed, and his skin is quite pale. There is a bruise above his right eyebrow. His shirt is stained in several places with a brownish liquid that may be coffee; it is not buttoned correctly nor tucked in at the waist. His pants are threadbare, torn at the knees, and a bit loose on him. He is also wearing bedroom slippers made of pink terry cloth and walks with an odd gait, as if on tip-toe. In one hand, he is holding an old fashioned cell phone. In the other hand, he is carrying a partially open brown duffle bag and, as he approaches other pedestrians, he uses both hands to pull the bag in close to his body. He seems to become tense and shouts repeatedly, "DON'T LOOK IN MY BAG! DON'T LOOK IN MY BAG!!" As he passes you, you glance at him and his bag. In the bag you see what looks like an enormous collection of old cheap pens and worn down pencils, mixed with jelly beans.

Question: Which behaviors described above demonstrate each of the following concepts?

- average (ordinary, typical) behavior
- deviation from average behavior
- ideal behavior
- deviation from ideal behavior
- a sense of personal comfort
- a sense of personal discomfort (subjective distress)
- effective functioning
- an inability to function effectively

Question: How would each of the following perspectives explain the behaviors described above?

- trait theorist
- learning (experiential) perspective
- humanistic perspective
- psychodynamic perspective

know it. More specifically, Rogers suggested that lack of congruence (i.e., incongruity between the ideal self and the actual self) leads to subjective distress, which often prompts individuals to seek psychological help.

Psychodynamic Perspectives on Abnormal Behavior

Psychodynamic theorists believe that most behavior derives from unconscious causes. They assert that aspects of personality—specifically the id, ego, and superego—vie with each other to control our behavior in ways that satisfy urges, operate realistically, or abide by moral standards, respectively. According to this complicated perspective, abnormal behavior can develop in a number of ways.

One way to account for abnormal behavior involves the proportionate sizes of the three aspects of personality. A component that is comparatively large overshadows the other components and its agenda dominates personality to such an extent that behavior becomes disordered. For example, an over developed id—whose blatant wants and urges are not constrained by a strong ego or powerful superego—produces a personality that is demanding, impatient, and unsympathetic. It is a short step from this personality structure to behavioral signs of the imbalance that may include stomping out of a bank when the line of customers moves very slowly, for example.

Another way that abnormal behavior may surface stems from anomalies in psychosexual development. As described more fully in Chapter 1, poor resolution of crucial conflicts results in a fixation of psychic energy (libido) that essentially remains engaged in the original conflict. The ongoing investment of psychic energy in an earlier stage of psychosexual development produces symptoms that reflect the conflict. An oral fixation might express itself through excessive oral activities that comprise relatively normal behaviors (e.g., gum chewing or talking a great deal) or abnormal behaviors (e.g., thumb sucking as an adult).

Because the psychodynamic perspective holds that all behavior is motivated and meaningful, this perspective gives wide berth to behaviors that otherwise might appear simply odd or peculiar. For example, Adler noted that an **inferiority complex** is an ordinary occurrence within one's development because **striving for superiority** is normal and failing to achieve it causes one concern. Admittedly, everyday use of the term "inferiority complex" bastardizes its true meaning. But Adler also posits that one strives for superiority not over others but over oneself, by working to accomplish the tasks and goals one establishes for oneself.

Similarly, Freud delineated a number of ego defense mechanisms to explain how the ego settles conflicts between warring factions of personality. Employing effective defenses is necessary and normal, and many behaviors associated with defense mechanisms and with fixations fall well within the range of normal behavior despite their psychodynamic significance.

CONCLUSION

Individuals with serious mental disorders may experience substantial emotional discomfort or mental disturbance. Moreover, their ability to manage important aspects of their lives may have deteriorated to the extent that they are unable to function productively in social, familial, or occupational realms. They may demonstrate peculiar or bizarre behaviors or behaviors that others find deeply disturbing or disruptive.

Because abnormal behavior affects many areas of people's lives, it is not uncommon for people to know one or more individuals whose behavior deviates from that which is considered normal. Furthermore, it is important for psychologists to understand aberrant behavior as well as its causes. But the process of understanding must begin with distinguishing disordered behavior from that which is not disordered. At the same time, it is imperative for psychologists to retain a view of individuals as whole people, with some behaviors that might qualify as normal and some that might be considered abnormal. Abnormal behaviors become the target of treatment efforts. Normal behaviors become assets in treatment as they shore up effective functioning and preserve self-respect.

Ultimately, viewing behavior along a continuum ranging from "most assuredly normal" to "most assuredly abnormal" rather than as a duality (normal *versus* abnormal) may capture more fully the relationship between normal and abnormal behavior. Behavior is dynamic and reactive to environmental as well as internal events. As events and circumstances unfold and influence behavior, its location on the continuum can shift in one direction or the other.

Further Reading

Baur, S. *The Dinosaur Man: Tales of Madness and Enchantment from the Back Ward*. New York: HarperCollins, 1991.

Beck, A. "The Development of Depression: A Cognitive Model." In T. Millon (Ed.), *Theories of Personality*. 3rd ed. (pp. 247–256). New York: Holt, Rinehart, & Winston, 1983.

Bernard, J.M. "Life Lines—Laura Perls: From Ground to Figure." *Journal of Counseling and Development* 64 (1986): 367–374.

Ellis, A. "Addictive Behaviors and Personality Disorders." *Social Policy* 29 (1998): 25–30.

Genova, L. *Still Alice*. New York: Pocket Books, 2009.

Sacks, O. *The Man Who Mistook His Wife for a Hat and Other Clinical Tales*. New York: HarperCollins, 1985.

Watson, J., and R. Rayner. "Conditioned Emotional Reactions." *Journal of Experimental Psychology* 3 (1920): 1–14.

CHAPTER 3

ASSESSING PERSONALITY AND PSYCHOLOGICAL DISORDERS

Psychological practitioners spend considerable time engaged in assessment related activities. The term **assessment** refers to a broad array of possible activities, all of which involve collecting, evaluating, and integrating data from multiple sources. The ultimate goal of assessment is to enhance decision making. In the context of personality assessment and assessment of psychological disorders, the assessment process often provides a description (e.g., of intelligence level) and a prediction (e.g., concerning the level of academic achievement an individual is likely to demonstrate). The description and the prediction facilitate good decision making (e.g., with regard to the academic placement that is best for this individual).

In abnormal psychology, decision making may involve rendering a diagnosis (see Chapter 4) or identifying appropriate treatment options (see Chapter 5). In personality assessment, results may be used to determine who is most suitable for specific jobs that entail great risk or great pressure (e.g., nuclear power plant engineer, police officer).

THE NATURE OF PSYCHOLOGICAL TESTS

Assessment activities often include the use of formal tests, which can facilitate a comprehensive understanding of an individual or some important aspect of that individual. Psychological tests are standard measures intended to provide information about specific features of individuals being tested. Psychologists use tests to measure a variety of phenomena, including personality, achievement, ability, intelligence, interests, as well as knowledge and skill in specific subject areas.

In most situations, tests do not cover every aspect of the area they assess. Tests are not designed to contain every conceivable question that could be asked in a given area of interest. Instead, they are designed to take a sample of whatever behavior or characteristic they target to estimate test takers' performance levels in that target area. Thus, a **test** represents a sample of behavior, taken at a particular point in time, under particular circumstances.

When a test taker retakes a test at a *different* point in time, under *different* circumstances, his or her test scores may differ somewhat from the initial results. For good tests, these differences are typically small, which indicates stability of the test scores. As an analogy, think about weighing yourself on your own bathroom scale at home one morning and then again after you return home from a busy day. Although the time and circumstances differ, you nevertheless expect your weight to vary by no more than a pound or two.

Understanding Test Formats and Norms

Tests differ appreciably in the format used to sample behaviors. Some rely on the test taker to provide answers, without guidance or prompting from a professional psychologist. For obvious reasons, this test format is called **self-report**. Often, self-report measures use a paper-and-pencil format that requires the test taker to fill in an oval (bubble) on a form (bubble sheet). The form is then scanned by an optical scanning machine to determine the scores.

Other tests are designed for administration by a testing professional, such as an appropriately trained psychologist. Generally, such tests are administrated on an individual basis. These tests are called **standardized tests** because they depend upon strict adherence to the test administration procedures, which are established during the process of test development. Standardization helps ensure that test takers are treated in an identical—and therefore fair—manner.

Once the scores of individual test takers on these standardized tests are collected, tests results for individual test takers are compared with average results obtained by a larger group of test takers to determine an individual test taker's relative standing. The larger group used for comparison comprises a **standardization sample.** Individuals in this sample group participated in the test development process by taking the final version of the test, just prior to its release.

The standardization sample must include participants from as many diverse demographic groups as possible, in proportion to their numbers within the population with whom the test will be used. Using a standardization sample whose characteristics mirror those of the group whose members ultimately will take the test helps ensure the test scores will reflect abilities and characteristics fairly for all test takers.

Many self-report measures rely upon a familiar pencil-and-paper format known as a "bubble sheet." *(Shutterstock)*

Scores from the standardization sample form the basis for establishing **test norms**—standards of test performance that comprise the basis for comparison of subsequent scores obtained by actual test takers. Test developers frequently

Many psychological tests require individual administration by a professional psychologist. *(Shutterstock)*

address certain test taker characteristics (such as age) that influence expected test scores by developing separate norms for different groups (such as groups that include people in a certain age range).

Properties of Tests

Good tests must demonstrate that they produce dependable results and that their scores accurately reflect that which is being assessed. The degree to which a test produces dependable results indicates the test's **reliability.** For example, if an examinee retakes a personality test a few weeks after having taken the test the first time, the score obtained on the second administration should be essentially the same as the score obtained for the first administration. The mere passage of time should not alter the test results. This kind of reliability is called **test-retest reliability.**

Another approach to evaluating a test's reliability depends on the use of different raters or scorers. In this case, an examinee takes a test and two different psychologists score the test. Again, the two scores should be essentially the same. The test score should be independent of the person who scores the test. This kind of reliability is called **interrater** (or **interscorer**) **reliability.**

A somewhat more complicated approach to test reliability examines score consistency by splitting the test into two parts. One simple way to accomplish this task is to divide the test by item numbers into halves, using even-numbered and odd-numbered items to form the two halves. Scores are computed for each half of the test across a number of test takers. Scores derived from the even-numbered half-test should be closely aligned with scores derived from the odd-numbered half-test. One expects the two halves to yield essentially the same score. This kind of reliability is called **split-half reliability**. Split-half reliability is a type of **internal consistency reliability,** which evaluates the extent to which a test's items work as a unified group to assess a specific construct.

The degree to which a test's scores reflect the behavior or characteristic it purports to measure indicates the test's **validity**. Test authors and publishers must present evidence of a test's validity in order for test users to be confident that the scores generated may be used in the manner claimed by the test author or publisher. For example, a test author who claims that his or her test measures intelligence must offer evidence that supports this claim. Without such evidence, the scores have no applicability. For example, in the absence of validity evidence, test scores cannot be used to support decisions about placing a particular student into a special educational setting. Validity *evidence* may take different forms, but all evidence serves a single purpose—to support a test's construct validity. For example, if a given test purports to measure the construct of intelligence, then its scores should align with scores obtained from an existing measure with a proven track record for measuring intelligence. On the other hand, its scores should not align with scores obtained from an existing measure that is known to measure something other than intelligence. For the test scores to be useful, they must capture the construct of interest, not something else.

So one kind of validity evidence may derive from studies that consider how well results obtained from a newly published test agree with results obtained from an established test that is recognized as a standard within the field. Another way to provide validity evidence involves using test scores to predict performance in a related area. Test scores that predict subsequent performance accurately offer compelling validity evidence and can therefore be used in the manner the test publisher or author suggests.

ASSESSMENT METHODS

Assessment methods in psychology vary in the degree to which they employ structure. Most practitioners use techniques that have at least some structure, and some use highly structured techniques. Highly structured methods connote a high level of precision that might seem irresistible to psychologists whose scientific training positions them to favor evidence over impressions. But, as described more fully in Chapter 5, the basis for effective psychological treatment includes the quality of interpersonal relationships between psychologists and their clients. Thus, when a person enters a psychologist's office for the first time, that person should encounter another person rather than a barrage of formal tests.

Intake Interviews

A common assessment method used by psychological practitioners as part of their initial meetings with clients is an intake interview (also referred to as clinical interview). This initial interview helps a psychologist to understand the nature of the issues facing the new client and the manner in which the client understands his or her concerns. To an untrained ear, an intake interview may sound a lot like a regular conversation between two people who have just met. A skillful clinician often makes the intake session unfold seamlessly. However the clinician navigates this first session, he or she invariably seeks specific information that helps create a description of the client's behavior and overall functioning.

Within this first session, a clinician must come to an understanding of several things: (a) why the client seeks treatment (e.g., "What brings you here today?"); (b) duration of the client's difficulties (e.g., "So this has been going on for . . . a little while, a long while, what?"); (c) level of distress experienced by the client (e.g., "On a scale of 1 to 10, how bothersome is this situation for you?"); and (d) previous attempts to overcome the problem (e.g., "What things have you tried to improve the situation and did any of these things help at all?"). The answers to these questions help the psychologist plan the next steps of an effective treatment effort.

Within that initial session, psychologists must also determine whether clients are at substantial risk for doing harm to others or to themselves. Typical questions might include "Have you thought about hurting yourself?" If a client answers affirmatively, the psychologist pursues the subject with follow up questions (e.g., "When was the last time you thought about it?") Evaluating a client's risk of suicide (or potential danger to others) requires the evaluation of several factors that can contribute to or mitigate (control or lessen) the risk. If the psychologist determines that a client is gravely disabled, hospitalization may be necessary. If, on the other hand, the client's condition is comparatively mild, the practitioner may recommend other approaches.

The interview process described thus far demonstrates a minimal amount of structure. The interviewer knows the areas to address but asks questions in whatever order makes sense to him or her and does not follow a script.

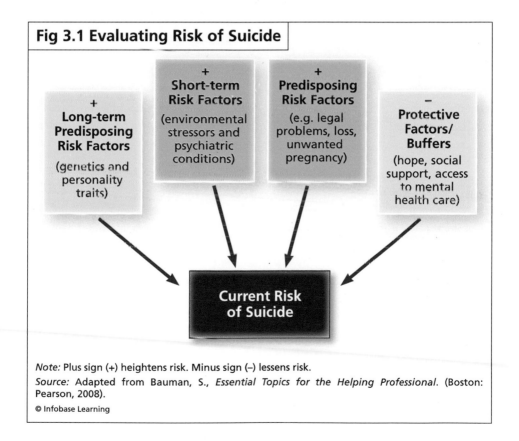

Fig 3.1 Evaluating Risk of Suicide

+
Long-term Predisposing Risk Factors
(genetics and personality traits)

+
Short-term Risk Factors
(environmental stressors and psychiatric conditions)

+
Predisposing Risk Factors
(e.g. legal problems, loss, unwanted pregnancy)

−
Protective Factors/ Buffers
(hope, social support, access to mental health care)

Current Risk of Suicide

Note: Plus sign (+) heightens risk. Minus sign (−) lessens risk.

Source: Adapted from Bauman, S., *Essential Topics for the Helping Professional.* (Boston: Pearson, 2008).

© Infobase Learning

Contrasting to this approach are highly **structured interviews,** which contain specific questions and procedures for recording responses and asking follow–up questions. **Semi-structured interviews** represent a middle ground between unstructured and structured interviews.

The Mental State Examination (MSE) comprises one of the best known examples of a measure that uses a semi-structured interview format. Some portions of the MSE involve observations made by the examiner, while other components involve questions posed by the examiner. The MSE assesses a variety of client characteristics including appearance (age, race, sex, grooming, manner of dress, overall appearance), movement and behavior (posture, gait, coordination, facial expressions, eye contact), affect and mood (outwardly observable emotional state and overall emotional tone), speech (volume and rate of production, appropriateness and clarity of responses), thought content (obsessions, hallucinations, delusions, thoughts of self-harm), thought process (presence of logical connections between thoughts), cognition (knowledge of one's own identity, where one is, and time; long- and short-term memory; simple arithmetic skills; general knowledge; naming objects; copying a design; drawing a map; writing or reading complete sentences; abstract thinking ability), judgment (ability to solve a common sense problem), and insight (ability to recognize the nature and severity of a problem).

A more structured version of the MSE exists as a shortened form of the measure known as the Mini-Mental State Examination (MMSE). The MMSE is a standardized measure for which norms are available. It consists of just 11 partially scripted questions or tasks that address aspects of cognition including knowledge, language, memory, and concentration. It requires only 5 to 10 minutes to administer.

Tests of Intelligence
Intelligence is among the attributes frequently evaluated by professional psychologists. Psychologists who work in school settings often administer an intelligence test as part of the comprehensive assessment required to determine what, if any, special services or placement a student may need. Similarly, psychologists who work in psychiatric centers, clinics, or other applied settings assess intelligence to help specify or clarify a complete diagnosis and to plan effective treatment. Measured intelligence comprises only one of several important attributes to consider when assessing an individual.

What is intelligence? **Intelligence** is the capacity to understand the world, think rationally, and use resources effectively when faced with challenges. Although some disagreement exists about how to best conceptualize the facets of intelligence, psychologists generally agree about the basic nature of intelligence. It follows that tests designed to measure intelligence need to sample behaviors that demonstrate one's (a) ability to learn and profit from experience, (b) ability to solve problems, and (c) accumulated knowledge.

A number of intelligence tests exist, each of which assesses basic components of intelligence in somewhat different ways. Some intelligence tests are designed for individual administration by an appropriately trained psychologist, whereas others are meant for group administration. Materials comprising individual tests are more expensive and the tests themselves are more time consuming (most take between 1 to 1.5 hours) than group intelligence tests. Various factors determine which format is appropriate to use.

Weighty decisions with substantial impacts on individual lives constitute **high-stakes decisions.** High-stakes decisions include those involving placement of school children in special education settings. Such decisions must be made with great care—there is much to gain from a good decision and much to lose from a bad decision. State and federal laws require tests used for high stakes decision making to be individually administered (and to demonstrate sufficiently high levels of reliability and validity).

Individual testing of intelligence dates back more than 100 years to the public schools of Paris, France, and the efforts of Alfred Binet. The French government commissioned Binet to develop a means to identify which school children needed special educational programs. In response, he and a colleague (Théodore Simon) constructed a test that linked specific abilities to specific ages.

In 1916, Lewis Terman of Stanford University reworked Binet's test and standardized it for use in the United States. The revised test became known as (and is still known as) the Stanford-Binet Intelligence Scale. Since its inception, the test has undergone numerous revisions and updates.

In its current form, the Stanford-Binet Intelligence Scale, 5th edition (SB5) consists of 10 subtests. Five subtests require verbal responses, and five depend on nonverbal responses. Subtest scores combine to yield a measure of verbal intelligence, a measure of nonverbal intelligence, and a measure of overall intelligence. In addition, scores from select subtests are combined to produce narrower measures (called indexes) in five areas: reasoning, knowledge, quantitative reasoning, processing visual-spatial information, and working memory.

David Wechsler was another major influence in the field of individual intelligence testing. In the late 1930s, Wechsler developed an intelligence test, which was called the Wechsler-Bellevue Intelligence Scale and was specifically designed to be used with adults. In 1955, the scale was revised and renamed the Wechsler Adult Intelligence Scale (WAIS). The current version, the WAIS-IV, emerged in 2008 following three additional revisions.

A downward extension of the WAIS formed a test appropriate for use with children from 6 to 16 years of age. This test, the Wechsler Intelligence Scale for Children (WISC), has been revised several times and now exists in its fourth

TABLE 3.1
Binet-Simon Scale of Intelligence
(1908 version)

Age Level	# of Items	Sample Items
3	5	Point to various parts of face
		Repeat two digits forward
4	4	Name familiar objects
		Repeat three digits forward
5	5	Copy a square-shaped figure
		Repeat a sentence consisting of 10 syllables
6	7	State one's age
		Repeat a sentence consisting of 16 syllables
7	8	Copy a diamond-shaped figure
		Repeat five digits forward
8	6	Recall two items (e.g., events) from a passage
		State how two objects differ
9	6	Recall six items (e.g., events) from a passage
		Recite days of the week in order
10	5	Given three common words, construct a sentence
		Recite months of the year in order
11	5	Define abstract words (e.g., *justice*)
		Identify the flaws in absurd sentences
12	5	Repeat seven digits forward
		Interpret the meaning of pictures
13	3	Distinguish between pairs of abstract terms

Adapted from: Aiken, L. R. (1987). *Assessment of intellectual functioning*. Newton, Mass.: Allyn and Bacon.

edition, the WISC-IV. A downward extension of the WISC produced a test suitable for use with preschool and early grade-school students (ages 2.5 to 4 years). Known as the Wechsler Preschool and Primary Scale of Intelligence, it is currently in its third edition (WPPSI-III).

A recognizable structure is used across all tests in the Wechsler intelligence test series. All tests have approximately 10 subtests comprising tasks that require either verbal or nonverbal responses. In addition, all Wechsler tests produce estimates of overall intelligence as well as scores or indexes of specific intelligence components (e.g., verbal and nonverbal intelligence).

Group intelligence testing originated during World War I, when the U.S. military sought to classify recruits for the purpose of matching their abilities to appropriate assignments. The Army Alpha and Army Beta tests were developed to assess mental abilities of literate and non-literate recruits, respectively. The creation of the Army Beta test was particularly significant because it demonstrated psychologists' early recognition that one need not be literate to be intelligent. These two tests served as models for the development of other group tests that continue to be used today in industry and in educational settings, as well as by the military.

It is common practice for school districts to use group tests of intelligence on a regular basis. The tests are administered routinely to all students in specific grades to gauge educational needs and progress. Among the measures used for

TABLE 3.2
Timeline of Development
of the Stanford-Binet Intelligence Scale

1905	Binet-Simon Scale used in France
1916	Terman publishes Americanized scale known as the Stanford-Binet
1937	Major revision published by Stanford group, together with two equivalent forms (L and M)
1960	Third revision published by Stanford group, collapsing forms into the L-M form
1972	New norms developed for the Stanford-Binet, using a standardization sample that accurately represented the U.S. population
1986	Fourth edition published
2003	Fifth edition published

this purpose are the Cognitive Abilities Test (CogAT, the modern version of the Lorge-Thorndike Intelligence Tests), the eighth edition of the Otis-Lennon School Ability Test (OLSAT8), and the Test of Cognitive Skills (TCS/2, the modern version of the California Test of Mental Maturity).

The construct of intelligence remains a complex and controversial subject. It follows that the best means by which to measure intelligence is also open to debate. Within these debates, however, there are some points of convergence as well as an ongoing impetus to explore new directions for test development. For example, psychologists agree that the domain of intelligence is large and diverse—in other words, intelligent behavior takes many forms. It makes sense that tests developed to measure intelligence should reflect this state of affairs and should therefore consist of numerous and varied subtests. Persistent criticism that intelligence tests overemphasize verbal abilities, for example, prompted the development of a number of nonverbal intelligence tests (e.g., the Test of Nonverbal Intelligence, TONI).

Psychologists also agree that most intelligence tests provide estimates of **scholastic intelligence**—intelligence reflected primarily in school-related activities. Some psychologists suggest that other forms of intelligence exist (e.g., emotional intelligence) and deserve more attention. Even amidst ongoing controversies that may include some legitimate concerns, intelligence tests are (still) the best means we have to estimate cognitive ability and to predict scholastic success.

Personality Tests

Personality tests measure characteristics rather than abilities or interests. Such tests shed light on an individual's emotional, attitudinal, motivational, and interpersonal attributes. Psychologists who work in applied settings such as hospitals, clinics, schools, or industry frequently use personality tests to enhance their work with clients. In treatment-oriented settings, personality tests can illuminate aspects of a client's personality that will help the mental health provider to render an accurate diagnosis and tailor treatment to the client's needs. In the business sector, these tests help identify individuals whose characteristics provide the best fit for particular types of employment.

As with intelligence tests, a number of personality tests exist. The tests represent a variety of approaches to personality in part because, as explained in Chapter 1 of this volume, different theories of personality provide varied explanations for understanding personality. The tests vary in form and length and, as with intelligence tests, are designed for individual administration by an appropriately trained psychologist or for group administration. The particular test a practitioner favors often determines which test is used.

Self-report personality inventories enjoy considerable popularity among psychologists and other test users. Self-report measures generally ask test takers about a limited sample of their behavior. Typically, these measures may be completed as paper-and-pencil or computer-administered tests that require minimal input or oversight by the examiner. Many test publishers of self-report measures offer automated scoring, which may enhance accuracy and certainly saves time.

Most self-report inventories comprise **objective measures** because they lend themselves to automated scoring—either by computer or by hand using a scoring template. In contrast, **subjective measures** require some degree of judgment by the person scoring the test and cannot be scored using templates or a computer.

The very nature of personality makes self-report measures prone to certain problems that do not affect other types of tests. Personality comprises a relatively stable group of characteristics or traits, but what belies this simplicity is that one or more of those traits may surface in one context but may not surface in a different context. This problem reflects **situational specificity**, wherein the way a person responds is influenced by the situation in which he or she makes the response. For example, anxiety about taking tests may cause great distress to a student in a classroom context even though there is no parallel level of anxiety during his or her completion of a self-report personality inventory. So the self-report mechanism used by this student in the context of "personality test" does not reflect what occurs in the "real test" situation in the classroom.

Another thorny problem that can occur in self-reports relates to the patterned manner in which test takers sometimes respond to test items. These patterns, called **response sets**, are systematic approaches to a test that produce a distortion of test results. For example, a test taker may respond to all test items by selecting the most socially appropriate answer rather than the answer that best reflects his or her true behavior or attitude. This particular response set is termed **social desirability.** It occurs quite frequently and may or may not reflect a deliberate choice.

Other response sets that distort test results include acquiescence and deviance. In the case of **acquiescence,** a test taker selects responses that reflect agreement with every item on the measure, even when these items do not reconcile with one another. For example, a test taker may endorse the statement "I am a loner" as well as the statement "I have many close friends." In the case of **deviance,** a respondent selects answers that reflect the highest level of deviance. Even true deviants do not uniformly endorse the most highly deviant responses!

The Minnesota Multiphasic Personality Inventory -2 (MMPI-2) is the most frequently used test of personality and provides an excellent example of a self-report measure. The authors of the original MMPI developed the measure to help streamline the process of diagnosing patients hospitalized in the 38-bed psychiatric unit of the hospital where the test authors worked. The authors— Starke Hathaway and J. Charnley McKinley—soon discovered the instrument did not facilitate their diagnostic work. However, they and their students subsequently learned that the inventory was useful for purposes of describing personality and drawing inferences about a person's behavior.

The MMPI-2 retained many features (and items) from the original MMPI. It consists of 567 statements to which a test takers responds "true" if the item is mostly true for him or her or "false" for items that are mostly not true for him or her. Psychologists encourage test takers to respond to all items and to use a third response ("cannot say") sparingly.

The MMPI-2 includes 10 clinical scales many of which continue to carry the names of the diagnoses originally assigned to them. Although the scales do not convey diagnostic information, elevated scores indicate unusual levels of certain behaviors. For example, elevations on Hypochondriasis (Scale 1) reflect higher than average levels of physical complaints, fatigue, and weakness.

TABLE 3.3
Clinical Scales of the MMPI-2

Scale	Name (abbreviation)	Behaviors Associated with Elevated Scores
1	Hypochondriasis (Hs)	Physical complaints, fatigue, weakness
2	Depression (D)	Apathy, moodiness, sorrow, dejection, hopelessness
3	Hysteria (Hy)	Desire for social acceptance, denial of problems, psychosomatic complaints
4	Psychopathic deviate (Pd)	Impulsivity, poor social adjustment
5	Masculinity-femininity (Mf)	Cultural, aesthetic, academic interests (for men); outdoor, mechanical, competitive interests (for women)
6	Paranoia (Pa)	Suspicious, sensitive, concerned with rights and privileges
7	Psychasthenia (Pt)	Anxious, obsessive, compulsive
8	Schizophrenia (Sc)	Unusual beliefs or behavior, detached
9	Hypomania (Ma)	Restless, distractible, high energy
10	Social introversion (Si)	Reserved, reticent, social discomfort, modesty, shyness

The pattern of responses obtained by a given test taker forms the basis for MMPI-2 interpretation. A test taker's response patterns are viewed in relation to response patterns from members of several comparison groups. The response patterns of the comparison groups were developed by analyzing responses to the test items and identifying items that produced different responses among a group with an established characteristic (e.g., depression, paranoia). Identified items form particular scales (e.g., depression, paranoia). A test taker's score on a particular scale is considered elevated when the score is similar to that obtained by the group with the specific characteristic of interest (e.g., depression, paranoia).

In addition to the clinical scales, the MMPI-2 includes several scales called **validity scales** that work to detect certain response sets. For example, elevation on one of the validity scales may signal that the test taker attempted to present a more positive picture of him- or herself than is actually true. Owing primarily to an innovation included in the original MMPI, contemporary self-report measures now routinely include validity scales.

Many alternatives to self-report personality measures exist, most of which require considerably more involvement by the examiner for administration, scoring, and interpretation. **Performance-based measures** (also known as **projective techniques**), for example, typically require individual administration that may include a number of verbal prompts or queries by the examiner. Several measures depend upon the examiner to record test taker responses verbatim (i.e., word for word). Given that many of these techniques also use a complex and time-consuming scoring system that cannot be automated, you might wonder why anyone would choose to use such techniques.

The answer lies in psychologists' belief systems about how personality is formed and how it operates. Chapter 1 of this volume outlined the basic premise of psychodynamic theories of personality. A core belief of the psychodynamic school is that that behavior results from the interplay among internal aspects of personality that, for the most part, reside outside of one's conscious awareness. It follows that psychologists who subscribe to this basic tenet believe that personality tests must tap a test taker's unconscious.

Projective techniques use test materials consisting of ambiguous stimuli (e.g., inkblots or grainy black-and-white pictures) or ambiguous tasks (e.g., drawing a person or completing sentences when provided with only a one- or two-word stem). In one way or another, test takers must organize and make sense of the ambiguity in order to fashion their responses. To resolve the ambiguity, they must draw on inner resources and project them onto the task at hand. In doing so, respondents unwittingly reveal important aspects of their personalities.

Examiners who use projective techniques provide extremely little guidance to test takers. They introduce the test briefly, note that there are no right or

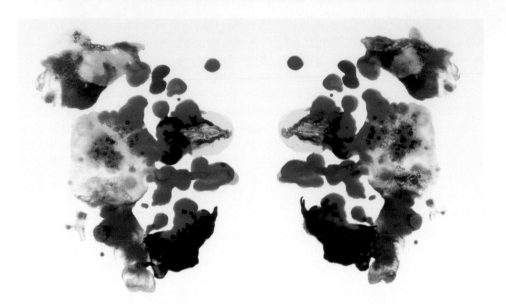

A picture similar to a Rorschach inkblot test image *(Spencer Grant. Getty)*

wrong answers, and present the first stimulus while extending an open invitation such as "What might this be?" If a test taker asks a question (e.g., "Can I turn it around?"), the examiner gives a noncommittal response such as "However you like." This posture pushes respondents to dig deep into their own resources for guidance rather than merely taking direction from the examiner.

The Rorschach technique is a well known performance-based measure that consists of 10 symmetrical inkblots printed on thick cards, one image per card. The examiner presents the cards in order, one at a time, and records the examinee's responses. As noted previously, the examiner gives little guidance during the administration. However, the examiner provides encouragement (one time) for the test taker to give more than one response (e.g., "Many people see more than one thing.").

Following the first pass through the cards, each card is shown again and the examiner reminds the examinee of his or her responses. The examinee must explain each response in terms of what characteristics helped him or her perceive that image and what parts of the inkblot were used to form the percept. This phase of administration, called the **inquiry,** makes it possible for the examiner to score the responses.

Several systems exist for scoring the Rorschach. All are quite complicated and time-consuming. In the most frequently used scoring systems, responses receive different scores based on the elements used to create a given image—for example, the shape of the blot (or part of the blot), color (e.g., "Those red spots look just like blood . . . "), apparent texture or shading (e.g., "It looks soft . . . "), apparent movement (e.g., "It looks like her dress is swirling . . . "), and content (i.e., subject).

The Thematic Apperception Test (TAT) is another well-known projective technique, consisting of 30 grainy, indistinct images, most resembling pencil sketches of one or two people. Typically, the examiner presents somewhere between 6 and 10 cards to the test taker. The examinee constructs stories about the people in the pictures—what is going on, what the people are thinking and feeling, what happened just before the pictured scene, and how will the story end.

During administration of the TAT, the examiner offers minimal guidance, other than to introduce the test, note that there are no right or wrong answers, and state the expectations of the test taker. Then the examiner asks the test taker to "Tell me about this picture." If the test taker omits an important part of the story, the examiner reminds him or her to include it (e.g., "And how will the

An image similar to those used in the Thematic Apperception Test *(Shutterstock)*

story turn out?"). The examiner transcribes the examinee's TAT stories word for word.

Several scoring systems are available for the TAT. Most emphasize recurrent themes and the overall tone of the responses. Some scoring systems identify test taker needs and motivations as well.

Clinical (Diagnostic) Measures

Clinical tests comprise a large and diverse group of measures intended to facilitate accurate diagnosis of mental health conditions. Diagnostic tests help foster the development of treatments appropriately targeted to assist individuals with mental health disorders. In this context, the overall goals of assessment include specifying a diagnostic category or diagnostic impression to be used in the formulation of a treatment plan that will assist the test taker (client or patient) to establish a more satisfying level of functioning.

An ongoing challenge in clinical assessment (and by extension, clinical tests) relates to diagnostic (or classification) accuracy. Detecting the presence of an existing mental health condition or symptom is paramount, so a test that correctly signals the presence of a condition or symptom demonstrates high **sensitivity.**

However, sensitivity tells only part of the story. After all, one way to ensure that symptoms are never overlooked would be to conclude that every case demonstrates the same symptoms! This is clearly nonsense, but it provides an easy to understand justification for why tests also need to correctly signal the absence of a condition or symptom—a quality called **specificity.** To be valid and reliable, tests must be both highly sensitive *and* specific.

Another consideration involves the proportion of errors (i.e., mistaken conclusions about the existence of conditions or symptoms) that a test produces. When test results indicate that a particular condition or symptom exists when in fact it does not, the error is called a **false positive.** Conversely, when test results suggest the absence of a particular condition or symptom when in fact it exists, the error is called a **false negative**. Sensitivity, specificity, false positives, and false negatives are all interrelated. For example, efforts to increase a test's sensitivity also increase the occurrence of false positives. Likewise, attempts to raise a test's specificity also raise the proportion of false negatives. Thus, sensitivity and specificity are best regarded as characteristics of tests that are not easily modified. Nevertheless, these features may prove useful in evaluating and selecting tests for particular uses.

Clinical testing relies upon the use of multiple measures to achieve its goals. Certainly, no single test can address all important aspects of an individual's life. Thus, diagnostic testing comprises a variety of clinical measures, including some tests and techniques (e.g., interviews) described previously in this chapter.

The group of procedures used to conduct comprehensive diagnostic testing is called an **assessment battery.** Assessment batteries are not uniform in content. Rather, they are customized to suit the needs of individual clients.

Many tests used within assessment batteries comprise **screening measures** for specific clinical conditions such as depression or anxiety. Such measures provide an overall indication of the (a) severity of related symptoms, and (b) need for further testing in order ascertain whether a formal diagnosis of the respective clinical condition is warranted. Many screening measures mirror corresponding diagnostic criteria contained in the Diagnostic and Statistical Manual of Mental Disorders (DSM). This manual provides descriptions of hundreds of mental disorders, together with specific criteria that must be met in order for a particular diagnosis to apply. Chapter 4 offers a much more complete description of the DSM.

The Beck Depression Inventory-II (BDI-II) is a well-known instrument that screens for major depression in people who are 17 years of age or older. It contains just 21 item statements, which respondents rate using a frequency scale corresponding to how often they experience the sentiments contained in the test items (e.g., difficulty concentrating or loss of energy). The symptoms captured in the BDI-II items reflect those contained in the DSM.

The State-Trait Anxiety Inventory (STAI) is another popular screening measure that assesses symptoms of anxiety in two ways. **State anxiety** refers to situational anxiety (i.e., anxiety that exists in the present moment). In this case, an anxiety response occurs in reaction to circumscribed events (e.g., tests, public speaking). State anxiety can be quelled or blocked by controlling environmental events. **Trait anxiety** refers to anxiety that is present constantly for a given individual and constitutes a personality characteristic. Persons with this condition may be described as anxiety prone because they respond with anxiety to any stressor.

Test takers who complete the STAI use a 4-point scale to respond twice to the same basic set of 20 questions. They respond once to indicate how they feel today (state) and once to indicate how they feel generally (trait). Scoring consists of a simple tally of state and trait indicators of anxiety.

CONCLUSION

The goal of all assessment comes down to decision making. Informed assessment practices facilitate appropriate decisions. Interviews, intelligence tests, personality tests, and clinical measures comprise the major assessment techniques employed by psychologists. Psychologists use these techniques to gather meaningful data that help them fully understand the people for whom they provide care and to render decisions that promote mental health. When used responsibly, well constructed psychological tests shed light on many important aspects of an individual's functioning. An accurate and thorough understanding is critical to formulating effective treatments for individuals beset by a mental disorder or mental health condition.

Further Reading

American Association of Suicidology. Available at http://www.suicidology.org.

Anastasi, A., and S. Urbina. *Psychological Testing*. 7th ed. Upper Saddle River, N.J.: Prentice Hall, 1997.

FAQ/Finding Information About Psychological Tests. Available at http://www.apa.org/science/programs/testing/find-tests.aspx#.

Hood, A.B., and R.W. Johnson. *Assessment in Counseling: A Guide to the Use of Psychological Assessment Procedures*. 4th ed. Alexandria, Va. American Counseling Association, 2007.

Joint Committee on Testing Practices (JCTP). *Rights and Responsibilities of Test Takers: Guidelines and Expectations*. Washington, D.C., 1999. Available at http://www.apa.org/science/ttrr.html.

Lilienfeld, S.O., J.M. Wood, and H.N. Garb. "The Scientific Status of Projective Techniques." *Psychological Science in the Public Interest* 1 (2000): 27–66.

Maruish, M.E. *The Use of Psychological Testing for Treatment Planning and Outcomes Assessment*. 2nd ed. Mahwah, N.J.: Erlbaum, 1999.

CHAPTER 4

CLASSIFYING PSYCHOLOGICAL DISORDERS

Behavior may be considered abnormal for several reasons and disordered behavior may take many forms. But although the overall concept of abnormal behavior is quite broad, a common theme connects its various manifestations: Mental disorders can be recognized by the high level of subjective distress experienced by the affected party or by the high degree of interference with basic activities that support effective functioning in everyday life.

Alleviating distress and enabling individuals to function more effectively are general goals of psychological treatment. In medicine, there is widespread acceptance of the idea that effective treatment depends upon accurate diagnoses. The same idea applies to mental disorders. To treat mental disorders effectively, we must first determine what symptoms exist and whether the symptoms point to an underlying mental disorder. Thus, psychologists use an organized and systematic approach to assess a patient's behaviors, with the intent of identifying (diagnosing) that individual's condition.

Efforts to sort or categorize behavior for the purpose of facilitating interventions have a long history. In part, this history underscores a natural tendency of people to try to understand others and the many ways individuals may experience life and attempt to cope with its difficulties. Efforts to relegate people and their behaviors into prespecified compartments have met with considerable resistance, a subject covered in more depth in Chapter 6. Here, however, we will focus on the pragmatic view that recognizes the need for a uniform way to assess behavior by evaluating and classifying symptoms. This approach parallels that generally used in all fields of medicine: To treat disorders, we must first know what they are. Moreover, we know them by their names.

MAJOR CLASSIFICATION SYSTEMS

In the United States, the *Diagnostic and Statistical Manual of Mental Disorders* (DSM) is the primary classification system used to identify/name psychiatric diagnoses. In other countries, psychologists often use the *International Classification of Diseases*, currently in its tenth revision (ICD-10). Chapter V of the ICD-10 is entitled Classification of Mental and Behavioural Disorders and corresponds closely with descriptions and criteria contained in the current version of the DSM.

As Table 4.1 illustrates, the DSM has undergone a number of revisions since its introduction by the American Psychiatric Association in 1952. The earliest editions of the DSM aligned with specific theories about personality or abnormal behavior and did not emphasize scientific findings. The third edition, DSM-III, was published in 1980. It boosted the manual's scientific base and moved away from previous theoretical constructs. The new conceptualization presented symptoms of mental disorders in objective terms, using frequency of specific behaviors to establish whether or not a particular symptom existed. If enough symptoms of a specific disorder occurred, the diagnostic label was judged to apply. Demand for diagnoses accelerated around this time as well, in

TABLE 4.1
History of Development of the Diagnostic and Statistical Manual of Mental Disorders

1952	The first Diagnostic and Statistical Manual of Mental Disorders (DSM) published by the American Psychiatric Association
1968	First revision, DSM-II, published
1980	DSM-III published with goal to boost scientific base
1987	DSM-III-R published, amid questions about diagnostic reliability, possible misuse, misdiagnosis, and ethics of its use
1994	DSM-IV published with additional emphasis on cultural influences on behavior
2000	DSM-IV-TR published with changes to text only; diagnostic codes and criteria were unchanged
2013	DSM-V expected to be published

TABLE 4.2
The Five Axes of the Diagnostic and Statistical Manual of Mental Disorders: Fourth Edition, text revision (DSM-IV-TR)

Axis I	clinical disorders including major mental, developmental, and learning disorders
Axis II	personality disorders as well as mental retardation
Axis III	acute medical conditions and physical disorders
Axis IV	psychosocial and environmental factors contributing to the disorder
Axis V	Global Assessment of Functioning (GAF; rated on 100-point scale)

large part because health insurance policies began to provide coverage for the treatment of mental disorders.

DSM-III established an important precedent for subsequent editions of the DSM. It introduced a five-part system (see Table 4.2) for describing and understanding an individual's difficulties and for predicting recovery. The five components of this system are called **axes;** because there are five axes, the system is **multi-axial.** This multi-axial system of classification expanded psychologists' view of difficulties experienced by individual clients/patients and allowed for a more complete understanding of these individuals and their respective conditions—both physical and behavioral. In addition to considering major mental health and developmental irregularities, psychologists began routinely to note medical conditions, psychosocial stressors, and previous levels of coping. The latter considerations helped to place a patient's difficulties in context. They also helped to establish realistic expectations for treatment, with a reasonable degree of hope for patients to attain a full or partial return to previous levels of functioning.

In its current edition (DSM-IV-TR), the Diagnostic and Statistical Manual contains descriptive and diagnostic elements for more than 200 distinct categories of mental disorder. There is a narrative description of the essential features of each disorder, including recognizable symptoms of behavior and additional information that provides a comprehensive picture of the disorder by describing how the disorder typically develops, the degree of disruption that accompanies the disorder, predisposing factors, associated features, frequency of occurrence in family members, and how to distinguish the disorder from other disorders in which similar behaviors may be observed (**differential diagnosis**). Highly specific criteria for diagnosing the disorder follow the narrative introduction.

The criteria spell out how many behaviors (symptoms) must be present, which behaviors (symptoms) must be present, how frequently the behaviors (symptoms) must occur, and the duration over which the behaviors (symptoms) must occur in order to warrant the respective diagnosis.

The DSM focuses on describing anomalous behaviors and does not attempt to ascribe causes of the problematic behaviors. Thus, its descriptive diagnoses can facilitate communication among a variety of mental health care providers, each of whom employs a different approach to address mental health problems. For example, psychiatrists tend to use prescriptive medications to control symptoms whereas psychologists tend to use psychotherapy to alleviate distress. As we will see in Chapter 5, effective treatment often involves multiple intervention strategies.

MAJOR CATEGORIES OF PSYCHOLOGICAL DISORDERS

The number of disorders described in detail in the DSM is far too large to allow for the present discussion to cover all of them, even briefly. The following sections focus on six major and relatively common categories of mental disorders: (a) Disorders Usually First Diagnosed in Infancy, Childhood, or Adolescence; (b) Personality Disorders; (c) Mood Disorders; (d) Anxiety Disorders; (e) Substance-related Disorders; and (f) Schizophrenia and Other Psychotic Disorders. A more comprehensive list is provided in Table 4.3.

Although the categories are discussed separately, individuals who meet the diagnostic criteria for more than one disorder are diagnosed with more than one disorder. This approach helps to ensure that treatment will be afforded in all areas where it is needed.

Disorders Usually First Diagnosed in Infancy, Childhood, or Adolescence

Many people would prefer to hold onto fond recollections of childhood as a time when life was happy and uncomplicated. But the evidence tells a somewhat different story for a great number of children. The children in question may struggle to reach developmental milestones or to achieve at grade level in school because of pervasive delays in development or more circumscribed problems, which can include delays in cognitive development, disorders in cognitive processing, attention difficulties, communication or motor skills problems, disruptive behaviors, eating or sleep disorders, and other problems.

Despite the name of this section, childhood disorders are not restricted to children and adolescents, nor are children immune to disorders that usually first occur in adulthood. Adults who meet the criteria for disorders that appear in this section should be diagnosed and treated accordingly. This recommendation is reasonable because disorders that escaped notice early on may cause considerable distress later on. For example, mild learning disorders may go

TABLE 4.3
Major Categories of Mental Disorders Included in the Diagnostic and Statistical Manual of Mental Disorders*

- Disorders Usually First Diagnosed in Infancy, Childhood, or Adolescence
- Personality Disorders
- Mood Disorders
- Anxiety Disorders
- Substance-related Disorders
- Schizophrenia and Other Psychotic Disorders
- Delirium, Dementia, and Amnesia, and Other Cognitive Disorders
- Mental Disorders Due to a General Medical Condition
- Somatoform Disorders
- Factitious Disorders
- Dissociative Disorders
- Sexual and Gender Identity Disorders
- Eating Disorders
- Sleep Disorders
- Impulse Control Disorders
- Adjustment Disorders

*Fourth Edition, text revision (DSM-IV-TR)

unrecognized until educational demands become sufficiently high to impede an individual's ability to achieve. When students enter college, poor reading abilities coupled with increased demands for reading "on one's own" may prompt them to seek assistance. A learning disorder diagnosis may be warranted at this time.

In this section, however, the authors of the DSM focus primarily on diagnosis of problems that normally first arise during childhood. For example, learning disorders quite frequently become apparent during a child's initial attempts to learn certain tasks or skills, such as reading. Stuttering (a communication disorder) usually becomes evident as a toddler learns to talk. The following discussion describes some of the better known disorders of childhood and adolescence in terms of their essential features and effects. These are Autistic disorder and Asperger's disorder, attention-deficit/hyperactivity disorder (ADHD), mental retardation, and Tourette's disorder.

There is a well-known maxim that parents of newborn infants should be sure to count the newborn's fingers and toes as soon as the baby clears the birth canal. This superficial check seems to provide a much needed, though often short-lived, period of relief that an infant is well and whole and off to a good start in life. But the scrutiny does not stop there. Almost immediately, parents, grandparents, and other well-meaning relatives begin to monitor an infant's progress on many other fronts, looking for signs that confirm its normal development and normal behaviors. Among the most highly anticipated behaviors is the true (social) smile, an indicator that the infant is demonstrating a real connection with caregivers. The baby makes eye contact and recognizes special people by smiling, hand waving, and gurgling in response to "cooing" noises made by these special folks. Not surprisingly, one of the earliest and most devastating problems adults may suspect in very young children is the absence of anticipated **attachment**, a term describing the social connections and interactions the child demonstrates with important people in his or her world.

In such cases, parents may indeed have cause for concern as the lack of age-appropriate attachment can signal one of several disorders within the category of Pervasive Developmental Disorders, each of which is associated with severe and far-reaching impairments in important areas of development, including social interaction and communication. In some instances, development appears to progress normally on all fronts, but then a marked decline in social interaction occurs. Eye contact may diminish and ultimately fade away. Reciprocal interactions such as mimicking facial expressions may vanish. Specific diagnoses in either of these cases may include autistic disorder or Asperger's disorder.

Children with an autistic disorder experience great difficulty in engaging in social interactions that depend upon a give-and-take structure—for example, games like Patty-cake that require cooperation or card games like Go Fish that involve taking turns. These children often play in isolation and may use unusual objects as toys, for example, spinning the lid of a teapot over and over. Language is limited, noncommunicative, or peculiar; sometimes there is no language development at all. For example, some children with an autistic disorder may repeat a word or phrase that was just spoken by someone else in a sing-song manner that is devoid of meaning, a process termed **echolalia**. Routines seem to be extremely important to children with autism, and deviations from expected patterns may be met with great frustration and rage.

Asperger's disorder is related to autistic disorder in that both involve difficulties within the social sphere. Children with Asperger's disorder demonstrate what appear to be milder versions of the problems seen with autism and, in comparison, may have very good language skills. Although children with Asperger's may appear motivated to engage with others, their approach to such engagement can be peculiar and oddly self-serving. It generally comes across as socially inept or insensitive.

Another disorder that tends to appear early in life is mental retardation, the onset of which (by definition) must occur before the age of 18. A core feature of this disorder is intellectual ability that falls well below the average observed in the general population. A person with mental retardation who completes an intelligence test will score among the bottom 2.5 percent of test takers. The degree of intellectual impairment is used to specify four levels of severity: mild, moderate, severe, and profound. By far the most common is the mild form of mental retardation, which accounts for about 85 percent of all cases. Individuals with mild mental retardation may be indistinguishable from children not afflicted with mental retardation during the early part of their lives; they often develop social and communication skills that are within normal expectations. Children with mild mental retardation can learn academic content up to about the sixth grade level.

Chris Burke, an actor who is best known for his starring role as Charles "Corky" Thatcher in "Life Goes On." Burke has mild mental retardation. *(Photo by Scott Wintrow/Getty)*

Another core feature of mental retardation involves corresponding impairment in **adaptive functioning**, which includes skills needed to support and engage in everyday life activities. For example, bathing and grooming skills are needed to maintain one's health and to facilitate participation in the workforce and in social settings. Figuring out how to travel from one place to another (from home to work or to a friend's house) is another normal and necessary everyday-life activity. So is understanding how to use money. All of these behaviors represent adaptive functioning, because they help a person respond to routine environmental demands. Many persons with mild mental retardation are able to acquire these and similar skills, which allows them to function reasonably well in life, hold down a job and live independently or within supervised living settings.

Attention-deficit/hyperactivity disorder (ADHD) is one of the most widely publicized—but not necessarily best understood—childhood disorders. Among school-age children, prevalence estimates range from 3 percent to 7 percent, even though causes of ADHD have not yet been established. The DSM groups ADHD with other disruptive behavior disorders such as conduct disorder, which includes a variety of deviant behaviors that infringe upon the basic rights of others (for example, bullying). The common thread among disorders in this category is behaviors associated with them can cause serious disruption or pose substantial risks to children with the disorder. Children with ADHD may or may not be hyperactive and impulsive; some are primarily inattentive. In other words, ADHD takes different forms and is not always hyperactive or disruptive. Inattentiveness, for example, may be apparent in classroom settings among children who seem to be off in some other world. Although the children exhibiting such behavior are not being overtly disruptive, they are clearly not engaged in the learning activity the teacher is conducting.

Jim Eisenreich played major league baseball for many years, during which time his Tourette's disorder was moderately controlled. *(Otto Greule Jr./Allsport/Getty)*

Tourette's disorder is characterized by the presence of multiple motor tics and at least one vocal tic that occur many times every day for a year or more. **Tics** are sudden and recurrent motor movements or vocalizations. Tics may be simple (involving a single movement such as an eye blink or a single vocalization such as sniffing) or complex (involving complicated movements such as facial contortions or complicated vocalizations such as words).

Tourette's disorder is rather rare (it affects only .05 to .3 percent of school-age children), yet its impact can be quite pronounced. Vocal tics—a core feature of this disorder—and some motor tics are disruptive in educational settings like classrooms and in social contexts like movie theaters. It appears, however, that tics are not entirely involuntary and many individuals affected with this disorder are able to exert partial control over how tics are expressed. A good analogy is the voluntary-involuntary nature of sneezing, which is essentially involuntary but sometimes can be stifled or postponed (voluntary).

Personality Disorders

As described in Chapter 1, **personality** is a stable feature of an individual and remains relatively consistent across time and circumstances. It represents an enduring pattern of inner experiences and behavior that creates a characteristic manner of interacting with one's world and the people in it. Personality governs the way we perceive and interpret people and events. It explains our behavior toward other people and shapes the nature of our emotional responsiveness.

In the course of everyday life, we encounter a variety of people, each of whom has a unique personality. Among these distinct personalities, some may strike us as rather drab and ordinary while others may impress us as colorful and outlandish. Sometimes we may experience an interaction with a stranger or an acquaintance and view that interaction as peculiar or even bizarre. We may be tempted to conclude that person's personality is unusual . . . weird . . . abnormal. But is it? And to what extent? Is the behavior we have witnessed extreme enough to be labeled "disordered"?

Personality is considered disordered when it deviates markedly from the normative expectations of a given society or culture. Pervasive deviations may be evident in cognition, affect, interpersonal interactions, or impulse control. Personality disorders differ from most other mental disorders because an individual with a personality disorder does not experience distress as a result of the symptoms associated with the disorder. The individual's perceptions, interpretations, and behaviors are **ego-syntonic**, in that they are not regarded as problematic by the person experiencing or demonstrating them. However, significant distress may be felt by other people with whom the individual with a personality disorder interacts (family members and co-workers, for example).

The DSM provides diagnostic criteria for 10 specific personality disorders, grouped into three clusters. Cluster A includes disorders with odd or eccentric patterns of inner experiences and behaviors—specifically, paranoid, schizoid, and schizotypal personality disorders. Disorders within this cluster all involve unusual patterns of interacting with other people. Individuals with paranoid personality disorder have a pervasive distrust of other people and their motives, whereas individuals with schizoid personality disorder are detached and aloof. Schizotypal personality disorder is characterized by deficits in interpersonal skills accompanied by a reduced ability to form close relationships. Behavioral eccentricities may also be evident.

Cluster B includes disorders with dramatic, erratic, or emotional patterns of inner experiences and behaviors—specifically, antisocial, borderline, histrionic, and narcissistic personality disorders. Disorders within this cluster are similar in that they involve a pervasive disregard for other people, coupled with a high need for attention or self-satisfaction. Individuals with Cluster B disorders often seek involvement with other people and may initially appear to possess good interpersonal skills. However, they tend to use relationships to meet their own needs for power and control (antisocial), attachment (borderline), attention (histrionic), or adulation (narcissistic).

Cluster C includes disorders with anxious or fearful patterns of inner experiences and behaviors—specifically, avoidant, obsessive-compulsive, and dependent personality disorders. Fear and anxiety about matters related to interpersonal contact form the basis for disorders within this cluster and influence the behaviors of individuals with Cluster C disorders. Individuals with avoidant personality disorder ward off feelings of social inadequacy and fear of being evaluated by avoiding activities that place them within a social context where such judgments might occur. Individuals with obsessive-compulsive personality disorder seek to achieve order and control over aspects of their environment that are unrelated to interpersonal areas, perhaps as a means of managing interpersonal anxieties. Individuals with dependent personality disorder relinquish all decision making to another party. They are submissive, passive, and dependent. Although they have given up control of their lives, they also have given away the anxiety that accompanies making decisions.

Mood Disorders

We use the word "mood" frequently in everyday life. We may notice, for example, that a co-worker seems to be in a "bad mood" or we may observe that a sunny, warm, spring day has put us in a "good mood." Sometimes, our mood seems connected to specific events, worsening upon learning of the death of a relative or friend or improving during a festive party. At other times, mood seems unrelated to what is taking place around us, as when we experience a sense of great contentment (or a sense of sadness or apprehension) for no apparent reason.

Psychologists expect mood to vary in the ways described above. Ordinarily, mood runs the gamut from feeling somewhat sad or glum to feeling happy or enthusiastic. Mood is expected to ebb and flow; in fact, a variety of mood states can emerge across a given day or week. Nonetheless, to some degree, mood should correspond with what is going on in the environment. For example, during an evacuation brought on by a hurricane warning, one's mood would be expected to reflect apprehension and concern rather than elation and silliness. In short, mood is expected to (a) vary, (b) reflect a range of feeling states, and (c) agree with environmental circumstances.

An essential feature of all mood disorders is a disturbance in mood, which may occur along any of the three core features described above. Mood that does not vary, does not demonstrate a relatively wide range, or that is inappropriate to the surrounding circumstances is considered disordered. Mood disorders brought on by a medical condition or by substance use make up a portion of the overall group of mood disorders. Otherwise, mood disorders are broadly grouped into those caused by depressed mood states (depressive disorders) and those due to expansive or rapidly alternating mood states (bipolar disorders). Within each of these two broad groupings, a variety of mood disorders can be identified depending on the severity of symptoms and pattern of mood fluctuations.

Major depressive disorder is characterized by the occurrence of a major depressive episode, in the absence of any previous or current evidence of a manic episode. A **major depressive episode** spans a period of 2 weeks or more. During the episode, mood is depressed or there has been a (nearly) complete loss of interest or pleasure in one's usual activities. Other symptoms may include weight loss or gain, fatigue, trouble concentrating, feelings of worthlessness, and change in duration of sleep. Dysthymic disorder represents a less severe depressive disorder characterized by milder versions of these symptoms.

A **manic episode** occurs when mood is abnormally and persistently elevated, elated, or irritable. A manic episode has a reckless quality to it that may not be immediately apparent. At first, an individual in a manic episode may appear to be in an exceptionally good mood—highly energetic, cheerful, enthusiastic, and rather fun. However, the over-the-top quality of his or her mood soon becomes clear and often interferes with productive ventures at school or work, or within interpersonal contexts. If not treated, depressive and bipolar disorders can have very serious consequences, some of which may be life changing or life ending.

The euphoria seen in a manic episode is accompanied by other symptoms, such as grandiosity, lessened need for sleep, pressured speech, and an increase in risky behaviors (e.g., spending sprees, indiscriminate sexual liaisons, high-stakes gambling). A bipolar disorder is diagnosed when one or more manic episodes occur or when one or more depressive episodes occur with a history of mania. Cyclothymic disorder is a less severe disorder characterized by milder versions of the symptoms for bipolar disorder.

Anxiety Disorders

To greater and lesser extents, anxiety seems to be part of nearly everyone's life. We may describe ourselves or other people as "anxious," and we may experience anxiety under a variety of common circumstances. For example, students may experience anxiety when taking a test, while waiting to hear about college admission, or during a sibling's military deployment. Anxiety often represents

Case Study of a Manic Episode

Janine is a senior in college, majoring in cultural anthropology. After graduation she plans to go to graduate school at a prestigious university, where she already has been accepted.

Out of the blue, Janine realizes her true calling as a novelist. She decides, rather impulsively, to write a novel instead of the report that has been assigned for her anthropology course and is due the next day. She is so enthused and feels so energetic that she stays up all night, writing a 200-page manuscript. In the morning, Janine realizes that the plot is all wrong and the story needs to be rewritten. She shreds the manuscript and beings work anew. She likes the next version better than the first but still finds it is not quite up to her standards. Janine believes that a truly fresh start will fix the problem and, with her third attempt, she is more certain than ever that the story line will proceed as she intends. But no manuscript is ever completed and no anthropology report is turned in.

When her friend and fellow student, Jason, asks about her report and how she is doing, she becomes angry and agitated, accusing Jason of being unsupportive and jealous of her writing skills and future success as a novelist. She storms out of the room and heads for the car dealership where she decides to purchase a new Audi Quattro by maximizing her credit limit across several credit cards, certain that her future earnings as a novelist will cover the costs soon enough.

a normal response to a stressful situation. Some amount of anxiety actually tends to help us perform better at many tasks because anxiety increases our level of energy and alertness and thereby prepares us to take on a challenge. However, excessive, unremitting, or misplaced (displaced) anxiety is considered abnormal.

An episode of intense anxiety or fear when no real danger exists is called a **panic attack**. This phenomenon is not an actual DSM disorder. However, the experience of panic attacks serves as an indication that an anxiety disorder may be present. In order to qualify as a panic attack, an experience must also include several somatic (physical) or cognitive symptoms. Typical symptoms are listed in Table 4.4.

A person with **agoraphobia** experiences excessive anxiety about being in places or situations from which it may be difficult, impossible, or embarrassing to escape. Anxiety also may involve fear over being in situations where help may not be available should a panic attack occur. Individuals with agoraphobia tend to adjust their lifestyles to accommodate the anxiety. For example, they may avoid anxiety-inducing situations by not leaving their homes, which represent safe locations where procedures for escaping or summoning assistance are well known. Agoraphobia often exists within the context of an actual panic disorder.

With a panic disorder, anxiety is both misplaced and unremitting, and there is no specific trigger for the recurrent, unexpected panic attacks that are the hallmark of this disorder. Following a panic attack, the individual lives with a persistent concern about having another attack. During this time, the individual may fret over having another attack (e.g., unpleasant symptoms), what the attacks may signify (e.g., losing one's ability to cope), or what consequences may follow successive attacks (e.g., loss of income).

Fears associated with ordinarily benign objects or situations are termed **specific phobias**. These disorders demonstrate both excessive and misplaced anxiety because the feared objects or situations pose little or no risk to the individual experiencing the fear. Yet exposure to the feared stimulus brings forth an immediate anxiety response. The disorder is diagnosed only if it causes marked distress or if the individual's efforts to avoid the stimulus interfere substantially with daily life. A very extensive variety of objects and situations may form the basis for specific phobias. DSM lists subtypes by groups: animal type (e.g., fear

TABLE 4.4
Somatic and Cognitive Symptoms of Panic Attacks

- Heart palpitations or pounding heart or accelerated heart rate
- Sweating
- Trembling or shaking
- Shortness of breath, sensation of smothering, or feeling of choking
- Chest pain or discomfort
- Nausea or abdominal distress
- Feeling dizzy, unsteady, lightheaded, or faint
- Feelings of unreality (derealization)
- Feelings of being detached from oneself (depersonalization)
- Fear of losing control or going crazy
- Fear of dying
- Numbness or tingling sensations (paresthesias)
- Chills or hot flushes

(Four must be present to substantiate a panic attack.)

of insects, fear of birds), natural environment type (e.g., fear of heights, fear of water), blood-injection-injury type (e.g., fear of blood), and situational type (e.g., fear of enclosed places, fear of flying).

The essential feature of **social phobia** is excessive and pronounced fear of social situations, including performances, where embarrassment may occur. Individuals with the disorder typically avoid such situations. When almost any social situation prompts fear or anxiety, the disorder is considered to be a "generalized" type of social phobia. Both the fear itself and the avoidance maneuvers employed to avoid social situations that prompt anxiety may interfere considerably with everyday life activities. For example, an individual with a severe social phobia may be unable to go to work or school because these situations entail social interactions.

Obsessions are intrusive thoughts, ideas, images, or impulses that recur even though one would rather they did not. Some examples include persistent thoughts about environmental contaminants or repeated impulses to shout an obscenity. In some cases, the obsessions themselves are problematic (e.g., experiencing an urge to hurt one's child). In other cases, the obsessive thought itself is not problematic (e.g., thinking about germs)—it is the unrelenting nature of the thought that creates difficulties. **Compulsions** are repetitive overt or covert (mental) acts that one is unable to resist. Some examples include hand washing or praying. The acts themselves are not problematic. Rather, it is the relentless, irresistible need to perform the acts that causes considerable impairment. An individual who experiences recurrent obsessions or compulsions that are severe enough to consume a great deal of time or cause a high level of subjective distress may be diagnosed with obsessive-compulsive disorder. Although the obsessions or compulsions are beyond the individual's control, the person experiencing them recognizes that the thoughts or actions are excessive. Obsessions and compulsions appear to serve the purpose of quelling anxiety. Thus, anxiety increases rapidly when a person attempts to forego an established obsession or compulsion.

Delayed effects of a traumatic stressor may give rise to posttraumatic stress disorder or PTSD. Unfortunately, surviving an extreme trauma does not protect a survivor from developing serious mental health issues one or more months following exposure to an extreme traumatic stressor. Extreme traumatic stressors include experiences that involve death or serious injury (or threat thereof). Experiencing the trauma directly, witnessing the trauma, or learning about the trauma (especially trauma that involves a loved one) can produce responses of intense fear, helplessness, or horror. Subsequently, signs of PTSD may surface. These symptoms may include recurrent episodes of reliving the traumatic event, avoiding stimuli associated with the trauma, numbing of general responsiveness, and persistent heightened arousal (readiness).

Substance-related Disorders

DSM-IV-TR devotes over 100 pages to the discussion of substance-related disorders, more than it includes in any other diagnostic class. The extensive coverage stems from the inclusive nature of the term "substance" and the variety of substances that may form the basis for a disorder. In the context of the present discussion, a substance may be a drug, medication, or toxin. Within DSM, substances are grouped into 11 classes: alcohol; amphetamine (e.g., methamphetamine); caffeine; cannabis (e.g., marijuana); cocaine; hallucinogens (e.g., Ecstasy); inhalants (e.g., derived from glue, paint thinners, spray paint); nicotine; opioids (e.g., oxycodone); phencyclidine (PCP); and sedatives (e.g., prescription sleeping medications), hypnotics, and anxiolytics (antianxiety medications). Most of these substances come in numerous forms. Intake may be accomplished by a variety of means including ingestion, injection, and inhalation. In general, each of these substances may be associated with a corresponding disorder. Disorders take one of four forms: dependence, abuse, intoxication, or withdrawal.

Substance dependence is characterized by a group of cognitive, behavior, and physical symptoms, such that the individual persists in using the substance despite negative fallout. The individual often spends considerable time pursuing the substance and may experience cravings for it. **Tolerance** is a physiological process that occurs when a substance user requires greater and greater amounts of the substance to achieve the sought after outcome. When use of the substance is discontinued, **withdrawal**—another physiological process—may occur. Dependence can apply to all classes of substances except caffeine.

Substance abuse is marked by repeated use of a substance with serious adverse consequences, such as legal entanglements. The pattern is recurrent and maladaptive, often producing failures in a variety of contexts: on the job, in the home, at school, among friends. Still, the substance abuser persists. Abuse can apply to all classes of substances except caffeine and nicotine.

Substance intoxication represents an episode of substance use that results in a substance-specific pattern of behaviors, thoughts, physiological changes. Such episodes often relate to a substance dependence disorder or a substance abuse disorder. Intoxication applies to all substance classes except nicotine.

Substance withdrawal occurs when an individual who is dependent on a substance stops using it or greatly reduces use. Behavior, physiology, and cognition are affected, with the specific pattern of disturbances determined by the substance in question. Withdrawal syndromes often prompt considerable distress or impairment. Frequently, distress is so severe that the individual may seek to begin using the substance again, purely to alleviate the withdrawal symptoms.

An individual who repeatedly uses substances from three or more substance classes (e.g., alcohol, methamphetamine, Ecstasy) in approximatel

equal measure over a one-year period may meet the DSM criteria for polysubstance dependence.

Schizophrenia

Schizophrenia is probably the best known example of a psychotic disorder. The term **psychotic** implies a profound disruption of one's experience of reality—hence the phrase, a "break with reality" is sometimes applied to describe the psychotic process. As a group, psychotic disorders are poorly understood by the average person with little or no experience with breaking from reality. The severity of symptoms, degree of impairment, and pervasive nature of psychotic features may also compromise understanding by psychologists.

Most psychologists agree that the disconnect with reality that accompanies psychotic disorders is marked by the presence of severe sensory (hallucinations) or cognitive (delusions) disturbances. **Hallucinations** are sensory experiences that are not grounded in reality. In other words, the sensory experience occurs only in the individual sufferer's mind. The most common type of hallucination is auditory, with visual being the second most common type, although any of the five senses may be involved. Most often, hallucinations are disturbing or worrisome to the individual experiencing them. For example, a person who "hears voices" may hear a single voice that sounds like his mother repeatedly denigrating him and criticizing his every action. Rarely are the themes of hallucinations positive or pleasurable. For example, a person who experiences tactile hallucinations may have the feeling that hot needles are touching the skin all over his or her body.

TABLE 4.5
Subtypes of Schizophrenia and Essential Features

Paranoid Type	Prominent delusions or auditory hallucinations without disruptions of cognition and affect
Disorganized Type	Disorganized speech and behavior with flat or inappropriate affect
Catatonic Type	Pronounced psychomotor disturbance (e.g., immobility, excessive activity, mutism, peculiar movements)
Undifferentiated Type	Features of schizophrenia apparent, but criteria for the other four types are not completely met
Residual Type	Prominent symptoms have abated but some disturbance is still evident (e.g., flattened affect or odd beliefs)

Three times named Jazz Musician of the Year by *Downbeat* magazine, trumpet player Tom Harrell suffers from paranoid type schizophrenia. While he is playing, his symptoms are not evident. *(Tom Marcello. Wikipedia)*

Delusions are cognitive experiences, such as beliefs that have no basis in reality. These erroneous beliefs typically involve a misinterpretation of innocuous events. Delusions tend to follow a particular theme. For example, **persecutory delusions** involve beliefs that one is being followed, watched, tormented, bothered, tricked, or ridiculed and **referential delusions** involve beliefs that one is the target or subject of various comments, newspaper articles, radio shows, songs, newscasts, or book passages. In some cases, it is difficult to distinguish delusions from firmly held beliefs. In other cases, it is far less difficult as when, for example, a person believes that worms have overtaken his circulatory system and are now coursing through his veins and arteries.

Bizarre delusions, hallucinations, and disordered thinking (as reflected in speech, typically) are the hallmarks of schizophrenia. In addition, emotional symptoms may be apparent in the form of a flattened (unresponsive) affect, reduced speech, or lack of goal-directed behaviors.

Schizophrenia is a complicated disorder, with a number of variations in its presentation. DSM incorporates these features as descriptors related to the course of the disorder and with the identification of five subtypes. The course of schizophrenia may be episodic (with or without residual symptoms), continuous, or involve a single episode (in full or partial remission). The five

subtypes of schizophrenia include: paranoid type, disorganized type, cata-
tonic type, undifferentiated type, and residual type. All five subtypes require
the presence of symptoms for at least six months. An individual who meets the
criteria for one of these subtypes but for whom symptoms have been present
for less than six months would be diagnosed with schizophreniform disorder.

CONCLUSION

A classification system for mental disorders is necessary in order for mental
health professionals to communicate effectively with one another. It also helps
mental health professionals from different backgrounds to work toward similar
goals with similar conceptualizations of the difficulties experienced by people
with particular mental health problems. The extensive behavioral descriptions
of mental disorders contained in the Diagnostic and Statistical Manual of Mental Disorders provide an impetus for greater understanding of individuals with
these disorders. Although the discussion in this chapter provides only abbreviated synopses of several major mental disorders, the DSM contains descriptions
and diagnostic criteria for a great many more disorders. It is also important to
remember that a complete, official diagnosis considers additional concerns such
as medical conditions, stressors, and level of coping demonstrated over the past
year.

Further Reading

Chodoff, P. "Psychiatric Diagnosis: A 60-year Perspective." *Psychiatric News* 40 (June
    2005): 17.
Frequently Asked Questions About DSM. Available at http://www.psych.org/MainMenu/
    Research/DSMIV/FAQs.aspx.
Spitzer, R.L., and M.B. First. "Classification of Psychiatric Disorders." *Journal of the Ameri-
    can Medical Association* 294 (2005): 1898–1899.
Widiger, T.A., and L.M. Sankis. "Adult Psychopathology: Issues and Controversies." *Annual
    Review of Psychology* 51 (2000): 377–404.

CHAPTER 5

TREATING PSYCHOLOGICAL DISORDERS

Each year in the United States 11 percent of the population meets the DSM-IV-TR criteria for a mood disorder. In addition, 17 percent meet the criteria for anxiety disorders, and 11 percent meet the criteria for substance use disorders. Long-term (lifetime) prevalence rates are higher still, as approximately 1 in 4 individuals demonstrate behaviors consistent with a diagnosis of either anxiety or substance use disorders. Although these figures address just a few of the mental disorders recognized in our diagnostic system, the pattern is clear— mental health disorders affect many individuals annually and across their life spans.

Despite the prevalence of psychological disorders, many affected individuals do not seek treatment. In fact, of the people who meet the criteria for specific mental disorders only about one-third receive treatment for their psychological difficulties. Some sufferers may not know how to access treatment, and some may not have insurance plans that cover even a portion of the associated costs. Others may believe that they should be able to overcome their troubles on their own —that is, without professional help.

Some people who experience psychological symptoms may not even realize that there are treatments that can help alleviate their distress. But there are many, and they come in diverse forms. Available treatments for mental disorders include biologically and psychologically based treatments. Some involve prescription medications; others include **psychotherapy**, a psychologically based therapy in which a trained mental health professional engages a patient and applies psychological principles and techniques. Such interventions target psychological symptoms (e.g., anxiety, depression) and psychological functioning (e.g., cognition, attention). They usually work, and most people feel much better following treatment.

MAJOR APPROACHES TO TREATMENT

The frameworks of the major theoretical perspectives described in Chapters 1 and 2 (e.g., behavioral, humanistic, psychodynamic) form the bases for understanding personality and abnormal behavior. The underpinnings of these orientations also provide fertile ground for developing psychological therapies. Many of the major approaches to treating psychological disorders use the basic principles of specific theoretical orientations in a therapeutic (i.e., healing) manner. We focus the following discussion on several broad treatment approaches—biological, behavioral, humanistic, psychodynamic, and family systems—and specific therapies within each major approach.

Biological Approaches to Treatment

During the 1950s, drugs developed specifically to treat psychological disorders burst onto the treatment scene. These drugs—known as **psychotropic drugs** or **psychopharmaceutical agents**—affected patients' emotions, cognitions (thoughts), and behaviors. A narrower class of drugs, called **neuroleptics** (also called **antipsychotics**, or **major tranquilizers**) also emerged around this time. Neuroleptics were used to combat the most disabling conditions and symptoms involving severe distortions of reality (i.e., hallucinations and delusions; see Chapter 4 for further information).

Some historians characterize this time as a period when chemical straitjackets replaced canvas straitjackets. Psychotropic medications became the treatment of choice in many psychiatric settings because the drugs alleviated distressing symptoms and also reduced problematic behaviors such as agitation and aggression that sometimes accompanied these symptoms. In hospital settings especially, patients who were difficult to manage became docile and passive (and therefore more manageable) with medication.

Unfortunately, virtually all drugs—including psychotropics—may cause side effects. In the case of strong tranquilizers, severe side effects often occurred. Among the most troubling and dramatic of these side effects was **tardive dyskinesia**—a term that refers to any of a large group of involuntary muscle movements. A person with tardive dyskinesia makes repetitive and purposeless movements, many of which appear peculiar (e.g., crossing and uncrossing one's legs) and often involve facial muscles (e.g., grimacing, lip smacking, lip pursing, tongue protrusions, teeth clenching, chewing, rapid eye blinking, wincing).

As might be expected, some new medications were developed to treat unwanted side effects of neuroleptic drugs. In addition, researchers found higher

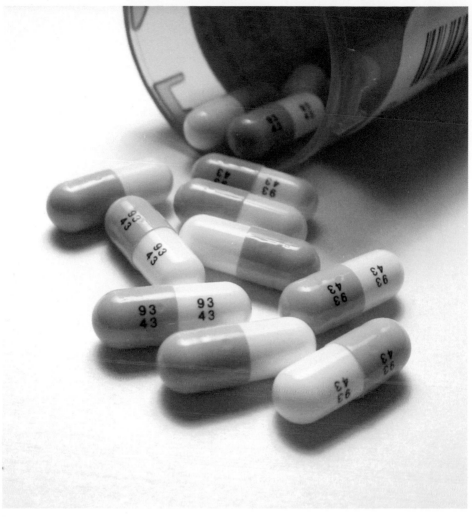

Prescription medication may help treat certain psychological disorders or specific behaviors associated with those disorders. *(Tom Varco. Wikipedia)*

dosages of neuroleptic drugs were associated with a greater risk of side effects. They then examined drug dosage levels to determine the lowest level at which the drugs were effective. For the most part, appropriate dosages of psychotropic medications reduced the number and severity many of the side effects.

Despite the drawbacks, the increase in the effective use of psychotropic drugs allowed clinicians to consider discharging even long-term patients. The Civil Rights movement that began in the mid-1950s gathered strength in the 1960s, fostering a growing acceptance of the idea that people should be allowed

TABLE 5.1
Sample of Common Psychopharmaceutical Agents

Drug	Brand Name/s	Effective to Treat Symptoms of
amitriptyline	Elavil	depression
duloxetine	Cymbalta	depression
imipramine	Tofranil	depression
phenelzine	Nardil	depression
tranylcypromine	Parnate	depression
clomipramine	Anafranil	depression, obsessions
fluoxetine	Prozac, Serafem	depression, obsessions
paroxetine	Paxil	depression, obsessions
sertraline	Zoloft	depression, obsessions
carbamazepine	Tegretol, Equetro	bipolar disorder
lithium carbonate	Eskalith, Lithonate	bipolar disorder
dextroamphetamine	Dexedrine	attention deficit
methylphenidate	Ritalin	attention deficit
pemoline	Cylert	attention deficit
alprazolam	Xanax	anxiety

to live life with as few restrictions as possible. Psychiatric drugs stabilized many hospitalized patients to a point where their release to the community became possible, even if there was a possibility that they might eventually require hospitalization again in the future. This movement, called **deinstitutionalization,** had both good and bad outcomes.

At first, patients who responded well to psychotropic drugs were simply discharged into the community to fend for themselves. Some had nowhere to go, and there was little attention given to easing their transitions. Some patients had become so accustomed to living in a hospital setting that they lacked basic survival skills. Many did not have drivers' licenses and did not know how to use public transportation; they did not own clothing appropriate for a job interview

buspirone	BuSpar	anxiety
chlordiazepoxide	Librium	anxiety
diazepam	Valium	anxiety
lorazepam	Ativan	anxiety
propranolol	Inderal	anxiety
chlorpromazine	Thorazine	psychosis
clozapine	Clozaril	psychosis
fluphenazine	Prolixin	psychosis
haloperidol	Haldol	psychosis
molindone	Moban	psychosis
olanzapine	Zyprexa	psychosis
risperidone	Risperdal	psychosis
thioridazine	Mellaril	psychosis
thiothixene	Navane	psychosis
trifluoperazine	Stelazine	psychosis
flurazepam	Dalmane	sleep disorders
triazolam	Halcion	sleep disorders
zolpidem	Ambien	sleep disorders

let alone an appropriate wardrobe to wear to work if they were lucky enough to find a job. Eventually, a network of adult homes, halfway houses, and related services were established to accommodate newly discharged patients.

Medications to ease or control psychological disorders continue to be used for therapeutic purposes. The caveat here is that they do not work for everyone, nor do they address every aspect of a condition that needs attention. Nevertheless, treating psychological disorders with medication can provide an avenue for relief of some distressing and otherwise unremitting symptoms. With this relief, people may find it possible and beneficial to engage in psychotherapeutic treatments that target other difficulties stemming from their psychological disorders.

Behavioral Approaches to Treatment

Behavioral methods for treating psychological disorders stem from the principles of behavioral approaches to understanding personality and abnormal behavior described in Chapters 1 and 2, respectively. In essence, behaviorism holds that behaviors develop as a response to experiences—that is, they are learned. And a simple corollary to this belief is that learned behaviors can be unlearned. To modify a given behavior, one needs only to modify a person's experiences with respect to the behavior's consequences or associations.

For example, psychologists believe that phobias form when something bad or unpleasant or hurtful occurs at the same time as exposure to a specific (usually neutral) object or the performance of a specific action. A person who has repeatedly experienced such a pairing, begins to associate the object or action with something unpleasant. Powerful negative feelings then prompt an individual to avoid the object or the act. If avoidance is not possible, the individual responds with high levels of fear and anxiety when exposed to the object or when required to engage in the act. This series of events is entirely consistent with the principles of classical conditioning, wherein behavior (fear) develops because of the associations made between an environmental (unpleasant, threatening, painful, etc.) event and a specific object or action.

Treatment of phobias capitalizes on the same principles of conditioning to establish a new association with the feared object or action. In **systematic desensitization,** a client with a phobia (such as fear of mice or of public speaking) is reconditioned to associate something pleasant with the object or act that inspires the phobia. To accomplish this goal, the therapist and client first work together to establish an **anxiety hierarchy,** by breaking down the troublesome experience into many smaller components. The client indicates how much anxiety he or she experiences with each component, and arranges the components in order of increasing levels of anxiety.

For example, a person with a fear of flying might use a scale of 1 to 100 to specify how much anxiety he or she feels when (a) purchasing a ticket, (b) packing a suitcase, (b) driving to the airport, (c) arriving at the airport, (d) parking at the airport, (e) checking in, (f) going through security (g) walking through the airport, (h) arriving at the gate, (i) waiting at the gate, (j) boarding the plane, (k) stowing luggage (l) buckling the seatbelt, (m) seeing the cabin door close, (n) listening to the flight safety briefing, (o) feeling the plane taxi to the runway, (p) feeling the plane take off, (q) watching or feeling the plane ascend sharply, (r) cruising at 30,000 feet, (s) watching the flight attendant offering refreshments, (t) returning tray tables and seatbacks to their full and upright position, (u) feeling the plane banking to prepare for landing, (v) feeling or watching the plane descend, (w) seeing that the plane is very low, (x) feeling the plane touch down, (y) feeling the plane rapidly decelerate, (z) becoming aware that the plane has arrived at the gate, and so on. The client and therapist work together to build

Fear of mice or rats is known as musophobia. Systematic desensitization is a classic conditioning technique that can reduce the fear by promoting association of the feared obejct with something pleasant. *(Wikipedia)*

an anxiety hierarchy that accurately reflects the client's experiences with flying. The hierarchy will not be the same for every client with aerophobia (fear of flying) as some clients are most fearful during the preparations for flight whereas other clients experience great anxiety while flying at 30,000 feet.

Next, the therapist teaches the client to relax every muscle of his or her body and to sustain this state of **deep muscle relaxation** for up to 15 minutes or so. This state of serenity is essential because it establishes a **competing response**— one that cannot co-exist with a state of fear and anxiety that accompanies a phobic reaction. Next, the therapist uses imagery to expose the client to portions of the anxiety hierarchy that engender very low levels of anxiety, confirming that the client is not experiencing anxiety and is able to maintain the state of deep relaxation. The therapist gradually ascends the hierarchy, exposing the client to greater levels of anxiety-producing images (although actual exposure is used sometimes). When the client reports any tension or anxiety, the session is terminated. Subsequent sessions will progress further and further along the

Fear of public speaking is called glossophobia. With classical conditioning, a therapist can help a client begin to associate the act with something positive rather than with something fearful. *(Shutterstock)*

hierarchy until the client is able to tolerate even the highest level of fear-evoking events on the list. At this point, the calm response has supplanted the fear response.

The application of behavioral principles to treatment models may include operant conditioning approaches as well. For example, **behavior modification** programs manipulate the consequences of behavior in order to encourage (reinforce) desirable behaviors or discourage (punish) unwanted behaviors.

A child who demonstrates difficulty sustaining attention while in school might receive a treat or special recognition after he or she manages to remain focused on schoolwork for 5 minutes. The reward serves to reinforce the behavior of sustained attention and increases the likelihood of its recurrence. A child who strikes another child might have his or her recess period reduced or withheld for a day. In this case, the consequence serves to punish the behavior of hitting a classmate and decreases the likelihood of its recurrence.

Token economies represent a variant of behavior modification and are effectively applied in community living situations (e.g., group or halfway homes or even within families) where residents must follow certain house rules. Adherence to such rules is important for a number of reasons: (a) to create or maintain a predictable, stable, and safe environment for all residents; (b) to promote the development of social skills that transcend the group living situation; and (c) as a means of ongoing assessment of progress that informs decision makers about

Parents often pick up a baby when it cries at bedtime. Doing so encourages future bedtime crying because picking up the baby positively reinforces (rewards) the behavior of crying. The parent's behavior is also rewarded and encouraged because picking up the baby removes the unpleasant stimulus of crying (i.e., negative reinforcement). Fortunately, the cycle (and the sleep deprivation it causes) is amenable to change through behavior modification. *(Wikipedia. Courtesy of Crimfants)*

who might be considered for placement in a less restrictive setting (e.g., supervised apartment or independent living). Token economies recognize specific desirable behaviors by awarding points symbolically—usually with something like pennies, checkers, smiley face stickers, play money—whenever a desired behavior occurs. Tokens comprise currency that may be redeemed for various items (e.g., coffee, note cards) or privileges (e.g., staying up an hour beyond "lights out" time).

Thus far, our discussion of behavioral approaches to treatment has centered on **overt behaviors**—behaviors that are observable by other people. But behavioral treatment approaches also target **covert behaviors**—behaviors that are not readily apparent to others and that take place inside one's mind (e.g., thoughts). In fact, some covert behaviors create a host of problems for people who seek treatment. For example, individuals who experience major depression typically demonstrate what some psychologists call the **cognitive triad of depression.** Sufferers endure unrelenting thoughts that they are worthless, the world is unjust, and the future is without hope. **Cognitive-behavioral therapy** uses behavioral principles to establish new associations to problematic thoughts (covert behaviors). In this case, a cognitive-behavioral therapist would address each area where flawed thoughts perpetuate depression.

Humanistic Approaches to Treatment

Humanistic approaches to treatment apply the humanistic tenet that people are innately good and possess an innate tendency to develop in healthy and positive directions that help them reach and fulfill their potential as human beings. Therapists who work within a humanistic framework believe firmly in the capacity and autonomy of individuals while recognizing that people may occasionally drift away from their natural tendency to seek to fulfill their

Rational-Emotive Behavior Therapy

Albert Ellis founded Rational-Emotive Behavior Therapy (REBT), a subtype of Cognitive Behaviorism, to address irrational beliefs that we learn early in life and internalize. REBT disputes the logic of irrational beliefs that follow specific events and replaces these irrational beliefs with rational ones. The modified belief results in a modified feeling.

Examples of irrational beliefs include:

- I must have love and approval from every significant person in my life.
- If I do not get what I want, it is terrible and I cannot stand it.
- People absolutely must treat me considerately and fairly.

potential. Departures from a healthy trajectory can occur because of brutal environmental circumstances that undermine positive pursuits. Therapeutic efforts are directed at helping people return to a natural, healthy state, often by focusing on their own worth, values, interests, and welfare.

Some individuals who seek psychological assistance appear to do so because of a general psychological malaise rather than a specific set of symptoms. During an intake interview, such patients may comment that "things just don't feel right to me," "I'm not sure what I'm after anymore," or "I feel like I don't know what I'm doing or why I'm doing it." They also may feel that they should be happy because they have everything they ever thought they would want—a steady job, nice home, and a life partner. These sentiments reflect that needs very similar to the lower level of needs articulated in Maslow's hierarchy of needs (i.e., basic needs) seem to have been met, but they also reflect a desire to satisfy higher level needs (i.e., growth needs, such as self-esteem and self-actualization). Because growth needs are psychological in nature, the therapist hearing such observations can understand the client's perspective but will not offer specific interventions that can alleviate the client's distress. Instead, the therapist provides an accepting, warm, caring, and safe environment within which clients may seek their own answers and solutions.

The psychologist best-known for a humanistic approach to therapy is Carl Rogers. Over several decades, Rogers' theory informed his practice while his practice informed his theory. Throughout this interplay, his core beliefs remained steadfast: People are fully capable of understanding and directing their own lives, they make decisions in their own best interests, and they are innately good, resourceful, and trustworthy. But what enables all this, according to Rogers, is reasonable environmental conditions.

One area where the environment sometimes fails people is in providing positive regard (i.e., warmth, respect, and acceptance). As explained more fully in Chapter 1, positive regard is most potent when it comes from one's self (versus from others) and when it is unconditional (versus contingent on certain actions being demonstrated). Unconditional positive self-regard is the strongest source of positive regard, but unconditional positive regard from others constitutes an excellent substitute source. Conditional positive regard sets up restrictions for receiving positive regard. These restrictions may be difficult to circumvent and can leave an individual vulnerable. In this vulnerable state, the individual may act in ways that do not align with his or her true being in an effort to obtain a few tidbits of positive regard. Because conditional positive regard depends on actions born of a desperate need rather than of a true expression of the self, its value is reduced. The lack of congruity between how one acts and who one truly is creates dissatisfaction and sometimes prompts a reexamination of one's identity and priorities. It is within this pattern of incongruity that the rationale for a humanistic approach to therapy can be best understood.

Rogerian therapists advocate **person-centered treatment**, an approach that respects the dignity and autonomy of the individual. Person-centered therapists believe people are fully capable of running their own lives. In keeping with this principle, person-centered therapists are nondirective, effectively assuming that clients are in the best position to know what they need from therapy in order to regain their footing. The therapist follows the client's lead, as evident in the use of techniques such as **reflective listening** (restating a client's statement in a way that demonstrates emotional understanding). Likewise, a therapist might remind a client of something he or she identified previously as something to address in therapy, but the therapist does not set the agenda.

In their work with clients, person-centered therapists offer **empathic understanding.** They demonstrate empathy by keeping their "finger on the pulse" of the client's thoughts and feelings as expressed in each session. This posture helps clients experience their true feelings and ultimately to resolve their feelings of incongruity. Therapists also need to exude **congruence,** a term Rogers used synonymously with genuineness. Empathy and congruence provide a firm foundation upon which to establish a collaborative relationship.

Not surprisingly, a key feature of person-centered therapy involves the provision of unconditional positive regard. Sufficient unconditional positive regard reestablishes equilibrium so that the individual once again acts in accordance with his or her values, interests, and welfare. In this way, the therapist fulfills his or her role: to facilitate the client's growth.

Gestalt therapy represents another treatment approach aligned with the general principles of a humanistic orientation. *Gestalt* is a German word that has no good English translation. It conveys the idea of a whole or complete entity that cannot be separated into its component parts without losing its essence.

Gestalt therapists emphasize the importance of fully experiencing each moment of one's current situation. Practitioners stress living in the "here-and-now" rather than the "there-and-then." They challenge clients to address moment to moment experiences while in session rather than to retell events of the preceding week. Because Gestalt therapists believe the whole to be different than the sum of its parts, they see no value in isolating behaviors or symptoms or viewing these behaviors out of the context of the entire person. Therapists guide clients to recognize what they perceive, how they perceive (interpret) that experience, and how these perceptions and interpretations fit with their entire being. As in person-centered therapy, an authentic relationship with the therapist is vital to therapeutic effectiveness.

Psychodynamic Approaches to Treatment
At their core, all psychodynamic approaches to treatment depend upon unconscious phenomena to explain personality functioning and aberrations of behavior. Therapists with a psychodynamic orientation believe that many

behaviors—including symptoms or otherwise problematic behaviors—arise from internal psychological events that occur at an unconscious level and therefore lie outside of our conscious awareness. Many of these therapists use techniques such as dream analysis and free association to tap unconscious activities. Dream content may reveal underlying concerns, conflicts, or unresolved issues. In **free association,** a clients reports immediately everything that enters his or her mind, without blocking (censoring) any content. With practice, this technique provides access to closely guarded material lurking in the unconscious.

In one way or another, all psychodynamically oriented therapists work to address imbalances among various aspects of personality or incomplete integration of these components. Their approaches vary in the extent to which they embody the original theoretical explanations proposed by Freud, although all theories within this orientation respect the idea that we are not fully aware of everything that motivates our behavior. Psychodynamic therapies that align closely with Freud's original model focus on bringing unconscious motives into clients' awareness so that underlying conflicts can be understood and resolved. Psychodynamically oriented approaches that evolved later on tend to deemphasize pathology (illness and symptoms) and promote **insight** and integration of disparate elements of one's psychic being.

Classic Freudian therapy is called **psychoanalysis** and typically involves frequent meetings (perhaps three times per week) over a long period of time (usually more than a year). Within sessions, therapists probe the client's unconscious using techniques such as free association and dream interpretation. Psychoanalysts place great weight on revelations that can be discerned from dreams. They believe the most important part of a dream is its **latent content** (underlying meaning) rather than its **manifest content** (surface level description).

But it is no easy task to discern the underlying meaning of dreams. A dream's content plays out intrapsychic conflicts between the id, ego, and superego, which are so threatening to one's psyche that the ego disguises the true content even in dreams! The content of dreams comprise symbols of pressing intrapsychic conflicts as well as people associated with these conflicts. The fact that clients' dream reports occur while the clients are awake creates additional distortions. While we are awake, the ego works to protect us against the turmoil of a dream's latent content and the anxiety we would experience should the hidden meaning become apparent. Thus, we often forget (i.e., repress or deny) major portions of a dream and we fill in the gaps inherent in dreams so the narrative flows smoothly—even though the dream did not.

Classical psychoanalysts attempt to play the part of a blank screen in their interactions with clients. At the outset of therapy, they observe and listen to the client's productions, but say very little. Later, psychoanalysts may challenge clients when the pace of therapy slows down or stops. These confrontations serve to interpret the client's **resistance,** which may reveal or suggest important conflicts.

Because the therapist maintains a somewhat passive posture, patients tend to relate to the analyst in a way that mirrors their interactions with significant others from the past. A patient who displaces feelings he or she has towards significant others and projects these feelings onto the therapist demonstrates the phenomenon of **transference.** Interpretation of transference comprises another vital component of psychoanalytic psychotherapy.

Few therapists today practice traditional Freudian psychotherapy. However, the foundation Freud established allowed for the development of other psychodynamic theories built upon his basic premises. Several therapies that developed later on gave greater weight to the fact that people exist within a social context influenced by the present day as well as by previous generations.

For example, Carl Jung's **analytical psychology** and Alfred Adler's **individual psychology** represent psychodynamic approaches with substantial contemporary appeal. Although Jung initially was one of Freud's disciples, he ultimately developed a theory and therapeutic approaches that differed substantially from those of Freud. Jung identified three components of personality: the **ego** (current thoughts, feelings, and reflections), the **personal unconscious** (stored thoughts, feelings, and memories), and the **collective unconscious** (a deeper, culturally determined level of personality transmitted from our ancestors). In terms of the therapeutic relationship itself, Jung believed in a warm and respectful relationship between therapist and client. Notably, Freud's relationships with patients were much cooler, in part because he sought to encourage transference (displacing feelings from earlier relationships onto the therapist) by sitting out of the patient's view.

Analytical psychology emphasizes intentional (i.e., conscious) efforts people make to integrate elements of their personalities. These intentional choices support the emergence of a cohesive sense of self that integrates conscious and unconscious aspects—a process termed **individuation.** Techniques to encourage insight vary widely and may include dream analysis, education, **catharsis** (release of pent-up emotions that provides an experience of relief), and **archetypal analysis**.

Individuation comprises a lifelong journey. One continually encounters new experiences and perspectives as the journey unfolds. In keeping with this idea, Jung suggested that midlife marked the first opportunity for full integration to occur.

Alfred Adler was another of Freud's contemporaries who parted company with Freud and established his own theory and brand of therapy: individual psychology. Adler stressed social aspects of behavior and especially the need to understand individuals within their social context. He believed early life events

Archetypes

Archetypes refer to the inherited, primitive components of the collective unconscious that have accumulated over the course of human history. Archetypes form scaffolds for personality as they provide a structure for the "building blocks" of life experiences. Some of the major archetypes proposed by Jung to affect the development of the psyche are shown below.

Archetype	Meaning
Shadow	opposite of ego, containing qualities the ego does not value
Anima	masculine side of a woman's personality
Animus	feminine side of a man's personality
Self	component that regulates personality and facilitates individuation
Persona	portions of personality presented to the world; essentially a mask that protects the ego

within one's family of origin provided the earliest social experience within which one developed a sense of self and one's relationship to the world.

According to Adler, an individual is the author of his or her life. Within this perspective, the therapist's initial role is to read and come to a deep understanding of the story. The behaviors a young child uses to navigate his or her life within the family context develop into **lifestyle patterns** that represent characteristic ways of behaving in dealing with all life tasks. One's most favored life style patterns constitute **priorities** or **typologies.** When confronting a stressful situation, an individual often uses a typology. Some common typologies include rescuing, controlling, excitement seeking, pleasing, and comfort seeking.

Therapists using individual psychology serve primarily as educators who help clients understand how early life experiences have shaped their personality. Family constellation, birth order, early recollections, and subjective judgments held by clients contribute to a **lifestyle assessment** that helps the therapist learn about a client. The therapist later uses this knowledge to craft interventions and to help the client gain insight. For example, a therapist may examine a client's **private logic** (the unique way the client understands life events) for disruptions and mistaken goals that lead to discouragement. The therapist then helps the client to reconfigure private logic and establish healthy goals.

TABLE 5.2
Some Techniques Used in Individual Psychology

Sample of Adlerian Techniques	
Confrontation	The therapist challenges patients to examine private logic, thereby helping them recognize that they can change their logic and, subsequently, their behavior.
Asking "the" Question	The therapist asks, "How would things be different if you were well, if you just gave up your symptom/s?" This question often occurs during the first session.
Acting "as if"	The therapist directs the patient to act "as if" he or she is the person the patient wishes to be.
Spitting in Client's Soup	The therapist points out the existence or function of a particular behavior and thereby undercuts its value. In essence, the therapist calls the client on a behavior that, once exposed, can no longer have the same payoff. For example, a therapist might say to a person with a simple phobia, "When you act so frightened of a little bug, you are calling the shots; everyone in your life has to be ready to step in and rescue you."
Catching Oneself	Over time the client begins to echo the therapist's observations about his or her self-destructive behavior or thoughts. Therapists promote this process by using the same phrase or gesture to signal each instance where he or she notices the behavior (e.g., "There it is again—you putting your needs on the back burner").
Task Setting	The therapist initially sets short-range goals that are readily attainable to ensure that the patient experiences repeated success. Later goals will be longer range and will be built using a step plan. (This technique is not exclusively Adlerian.)
Push Button	Therapists teach a client to recognize choices that can bring about desired feelings. For example, by pushing a mental button, a client can call forth a productive, positive thought.

Family Therapy

A mental or behavioral disorder demonstrated by one person may actually reflect a disturbance in the larger context within which that individual exists. This is especially evident when a child shows problematic behavior and families seek family therapy to address the issue, which they perceive as belonging to one of its members—the so-called **identified patient.** Families may enter therapy under the belief that family members can learn how to help the identified patient, only to discover that family therapy focuses on the interactions between and among all members of the family unit. Thus, the entire family is the patient. Like most unitary organisms, families try to preserve themselves by maintaining the status quo, seeking balance, and trying to reestablish a steady state (or homeostasis) as soon as possible after things have become unbalanced.

Family therapists assert that all members of a family unit constitute a system and that obvious problems (symptoms) appear in one member as a result of systemic issues. Such a **systems perspective** is not a natural fit in Western culture, which tends to overemphasize individual concerns. A systems approach does not discount the individual identified by the family as the patient because this perspective views the individual as embedded within the context of his or her family. Rather than being lost in the crowd, the identified patient is more fully understood. A family **genogram** comprises a common technique used by

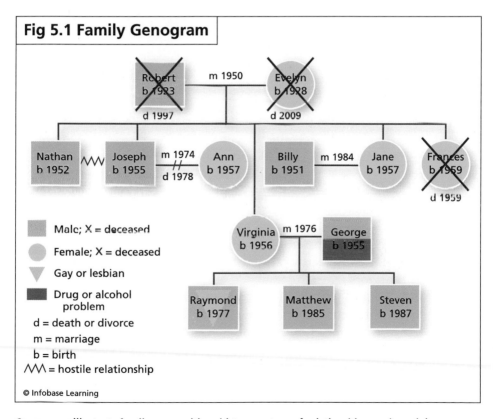

Genograms illustrate family composition, history, nature of relationships, and special challenges across generations.

A family functions as a system consisting of individual members and internal dynamics. *(Shutterstock)*

many family therapists to gather information about family structure and create a visual representation of the family.

Family therapists must keep several important considerations in mind throughout their work with a particular family, especially at the outset of therapy and when a child is involved. From a systems perspective, problematic behavior demonstrated by a child can

  (a) serve a function or purpose for the family (e.g., the child is the scapegoat, whose behavior excuses all other members' maladaptive behaviors),
  (b) be maintained by family processes (e.g., attention is focused on the child rather than on marital strife),
  (c) serve as a barometer of the family's overall ability or inability to function (e.g., when the child copes well, the family copes well), and
  (d) signal intergenerational dysfunction (e.g., alcoholism or sexual abuse that has crossed generational lines).

Family therapies have developed along several lines, with each applying a systems perspective. As a first step in the process, virtually all therapists form a relationship with the family by becoming a member of the family. Most therapists conduct a formal or informal assessment together with the family, as they seek to detect and understand the methods that family members use to communicate, preserve the family structure, and influence other family members' actions and growth. Initial observations usually include consideration of the outward appearance of the family, the basic feeling state, presence of repetitive or nonproductive sequences of words or actions, defenses used by family members, existence of subgroups or alliances, differentiation of individual members, and problem-solving methods.

Family therapy is a process, and the pace can become quite rapid, depending on the number of participants. Thus, family therapists generally become active participants in the change process, often using their immediate perceptions of the ongoing process to guide the process. For example, a therapist may interrupt an overly contentious interaction by saying, "Ouch! I felt the heat from that exchange way over here!" to help family members realize the intensity of what was said.

Many therapists consider the extent to which family functioning is adaptable (i.e., flexible, showing ability and willingness to change) and cohesive (i.e., reflective of engagement or emotional bonding between family members), because these are important indicators of a family's overall health. Although moderate levels of **adaptability** and **cohesion** generally promote optimal functioning, a therapist must formulate treatment goals that align with an individual family's preference. Family satisfaction depends on how a family desires to function, and culture influences the preferred degree of structure and

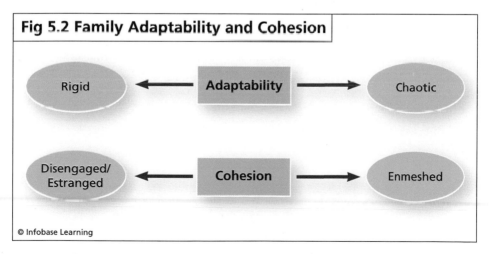

Family adaptability and cohesion are important considerations in formulating appropriate and effective interventions. Moderate levels of both characteristics tend to promote optimal systemic health.

engagement. For example, Amish, Orthodox Jewish, and Mormon families often show a preference for a rigid structure and enmeshed relationships but function best if all family members prefer this state.

COMMON FEATURES OF TREATMENT APPROACHES

Clearly, theorists and practitioners draw distinctions among the varied types of psychotherapies, distinguish one form of psychotherapeutic intervention from all the others, and endorse the psychotherapy that most closely matches their own understanding of disorders and how they are best treated. However, this selectivity diminishes a full (and potentially useful) understanding of the numerous common elements that psychotherapies share.

Virtually all treatments for psychological difficulties depend upon an interpersonal relationship that exists under a special set of circumstances. Unlike simple friendships and social or workplace relationships, therapeutic relationships center exclusively on the patient's needs. In addition, most treatment efforts share important goals: alleviating distress and restoring or improving a client's ability to function within roles and within society.

TABLE 5.3
Ethical Principles and Codes of Professional Conduct for Organizations Whose Members Provide Psychotherapeutic Services

American Psychological Association (APA)

Ethical Principles of Psychologists and Code of Conduct, 2010 Amendments

Published in 2010

Available online at http://www.apa.org/ethics/code/index.aspx

American Counseling Association (ACA)

ACA Code of Ethics

Published in 2005

Available online via www.counseling.org

National Association of School Psychologists (NASP)

Professional Conduct Manual, Principles for Professional Ethics, and Guidelines for the Provision of School Psychological Services

Published in 2000

Available online at www.naspweb.org

To facilitate their patients' ability to make effective choices, therapists apply techniques from specific therapeutic models that have demonstrated efficacy. Treatment does not involve merely listening, giving seat-of-the-pants advice, or telling others what to do or how to feel. Psychologists must comprehend, value, and respect a patient's perspective and experiences. Above all no psychologist should impose his or her own values on a patient. Instead, the goal of therapy should be to identify and implement interventions that incorporate a client's values and perspective. One important aspect of this construct is that psychologists should not recommend activities that are at odds with clients' cultural or religious beliefs or practices.

TABLE 5.4
Contents of the Ethical Principles of Psychologists and Code of Conduct. 2010 Amendments

Introduction and Applicability

Preamble

General Principles

Principle A Beneficence and Nonmaleficence

Principle B Fidelity and Responsibility

Principle C Integrity

Principle D Justice

Principle E Respect for People's Rights and Dignity

Ethical Standards 1-10

Standard 1 Resolving Ethical Issues

Standard 2 Competence

Standard 3 Human Relations

Standard 4 Privacy and Confidentiality

Standard 5 Advertising and Other Public Statements

Standard 6 Record Keeping and Fees

Standard 7 Education and Training

Standard 8 Research and Publications

Standard 9 Assessment

Standard 10 Therapy

Note: American Psychological Association, 2010, effective date June 1, 2010.

All psychologists are bound by a code of ethics that governs the work that they do, regardless of the particular psychotherapy they espouse. Across specialties and therapeutic orientations, psychologists adhere to five fundamental ethical principles that form the basis for the science and practice of psychology: justice, autonomy, nonmaleficence, beneficence, and fidelity. In practice, these principles demand that psychologists conduct therapy in a manner that respects the worth and dignity of their clients (**justice**). Practitioners act in ways that demonstrate an awareness of clients as autonomous individuals capable of making decisions in their own best interests (**autonomy**). Psychologists strive to avoid harming individuals with whom they work (**nonmaleficence**). They work to promote good outcomes for these individuals (**beneficence**). In their work with each individual, psychologists always endeavor to be trustworthy and reliable (**fidelity**).

In addition to the fundamental ethical principles outlined above, the American Psychological Association has developed specific ethical standards that provide a more fine-grained analysis of what constitutes appropriate, responsible, and professional behavior. Other psychological organizations distribute similar documents that delineate ethical standards. Although there is considerable overlap among these various documents, each professional association organizes and focuses the content to address its members' primary concerns.

CONCLUSION
Psychotherapy and psychopharmacology provide effective treatments that support individuals in their efforts to overcome psychological difficulties and mental disorders. This chapter described various treatment approaches, including a number of psychologically based interventions derived from various theoretical perspectives. Although the psychotherapies presented here have distinct features, they also have many features in common. Many therapists opt for an eclectic approach to therapy, a practice that involves selecting and using techniques from several therapies simultaneously.

Further Reading

American Psychological Association. "Ethical Principles of Psychologists and Code of Conduct." *American Psychologist* 57 (2002): 1060–1073.

American Psychological Association. Record Keeping Guidelines: Drafted by the Committee on Professional Practice & Standards, a committee of the Board of Professional Affairs, adopted by the Council of Representatives, February 2007. Available at http://www.apa.org/practice/recordkeeping.html.

American Psychological Association. Ethical Principles of Psychologists and Code of Conduct. 2010 Amendments. Available at www.apa.org/ethics.

Halbur, D.A., and K. Vess Halbur. *Developing Your Theoretical Orientation in Counseling and Psychotherapy.* 2nd ed. Upper Saddle River, N.J.: Pearson Education, 2011.

Henle, M. "Gestalt Psychology and Gestalt Therapy." *Journal of the History of the Behavioral Sciences* 14 (1978): 23–32.

Kelly, E.W., Jr. "Relationship-centered Counseling: A Humanistic Model of Integration." *Journal of Counseling and Development* 75 (1997): 337–345.

Preston, J.D., J.H. O'Neal, and M.C. Talaga. *Consumer's Guide to Psychiatric Drugs.* New York: Simon & Schuster, 2009.

Quick Reference to Psychotropic Medication. (2009 update). Available from: http://www. psyd-fx.com/html/quick_reference_chart.html.

Rock, I., and S. Palmer. "The Legacy of Gestalt Psychology." Scientific American 263, no. 6 (1990): 84–90.

Seligman, M.E.P. "The Effectiveness of Psychotherapy: The Consumer's Report Study." *American Psychologist* 50 (1990): 965–974.

CHAPTER 6

CONTEMPORARY ISSUES IN PERSONALITY AND ABNORMAL PSYCHOLOGY

The first five chapters of this volume discussed the various means psychologists use to understand and assess personality and abnormal behavior, as well as to classify and treat mental disorders. Within each of these areas, the chapters described current practices and respected theoretical traditions. But the field of psychology continues to evolve, and the scientific method that forms the basis for the discipline of psychology continues to inform psychological theories and practices. In this chapter, we will consider a number of special issues that influence the field and often generate controversy, both within the profession and among the public at large. You may find that you hold strong views on some of these contemporary issues.

MENTAL HEALTH AND MENTAL ILLNESS

Many psychologists who study personality or abnormal psychology tend to focus attention on aberrant behavior rather than on adaptive behavior because disruptive, disordered, or dangerous behaviors demand immediate attention. In fact, over the course of history, societal pressures often prompted classification efforts and/or intervention to remedy specific problems. As described in Chapter 3, for example, intelligence testing got its start in the late 1800s because the Parisian government wanted to identify school children who had special learning needs.

As the scientific discipline of psychology matured, psychologists became more proactive and less reactionary. They began to question why some people succumb to mental illness and some do not, despite comparable life experiences. New theories and clinical practices emerged during the mid-1900s, theories and practices that emphasized human capabilities and tendencies to develop in healthy, productive ways. Person-centered therapy (described in Chapter 5) emerged from this new emphasis. This therapeutic approach recognized people as autonomous, worthy individuals, fully capable of directing all aspects of their own lives—including their therapy. In 1960, Thomas Szasz published an important work entitled *The Myth of Mental Illness*. In this work, Szasz challenged the entire notion of mental illness, arguing that in the absence of a clear-cut understanding and description of mental health, we cannot presume to know what constitutes mental illness.

Following this rather tumultuous period, the discipline of psychology expanded to include new fields of inquiry that focus on positive elements of behavior and mental activity. Researchers and practitioners within these areas strive to understand mental health as well as how mental and physical health *and* mental and physical illness are intertwined. They use this understanding to (a) promote mental health, (b) avert mental illness, (c) foster coping skills, (d) encourage swift and more complete recovery from physical and mental challenges, (e) educate patients about how psychological factors (e.g., personality, attitude) and states (e.g., anxiety, depression) influence physical health, (f) formulate and pursue new research questions, and (g) identify and build on patients' strengths.

Health Psychology

Health psychology comprises a relatively new field that recognizes several influences on physical and mental health. Specifically, health psychologists employ a **biopsychosocial** framework built upon the importance of biological (physical), psychological (mental), and social factors in shaping our overall health. Indeed, many primary care physicians report that a substantial number of their patients' complaints have no biological (medical) cause. Psychological factors appear to be at the root of up to two-thirds of primary care visits.

With growing regularity, primary care medical facilities employ health psychologists to help patients understand the reciprocal relationship between the mind and the body. For example, research indicates that patients with unresolved anger or depression are prone to develop certain physical disorders including heart disease and cancer. Health psychologists can help patients recognize risk factors and modify behaviors that elevate patients' risk for illness. Interventions also may target coping skills following a diagnosis of a terminal illness or medical conditions that may be treatable or manageable but not curable (for example, diabetes or asthma). Individuals who effectively manage the psychological impact of their medical problems are likely to participate more fully in ongoing health care efforts. Chronic medical conditions and terminal

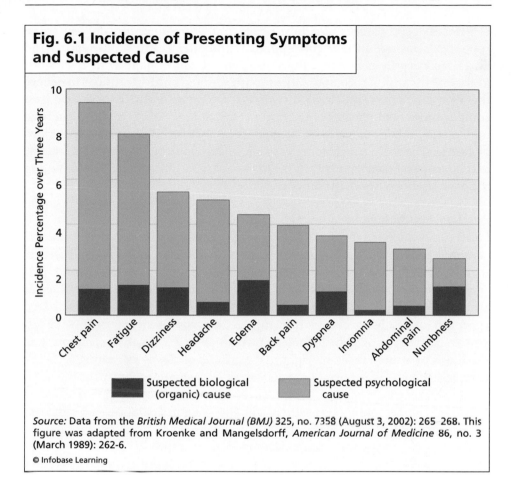

Fig. 6.1 Incidence of Presenting Symptoms and Suspected Cause

Source: Data from the *British Medical Journal (BMJ)* 325, no. 7358 (August 3, 2002): 265 268. This figure was adapted from Kroenke and Mangelsdorff, *American Journal of Medicine* 86, no. 3 (March 1989): 262-6.

© Infobase Learning

illnesses frequently co-occur with psychological disorders such as depression, panic, or anxiety, yet psychological aspects of medical conditions continue to receive scant attention.

Health psychologists also work to advance behaviors that promote health and, thereby, reduce the risk of various physical illnesses and diseases. For example, smoking cessation comprises a major effort among health psychologists. Smoking causes lung cancer and serves as a major contributing factor in heart disease and emphysema. In addition, it worsens innumerable other physical ailments (e.g., hypertension) and is suspected of contributing to the development of still other undesirable conditions (e.g., depression, accelerated aging, early menopause). In the face of such clear-cut evidence and flat out bad odds, it is difficult to explain why some people take up smoking and others persist in smoking—but health psychologists continue to investigate the reasons and use their findings to dissuade people from putting their health at risk in this way.

Health psychologists also investigate and promote optimism and social support. A positive attitude corresponds with better health status reports and faster recovery from illnesses. Optimism goes hand in hand with a "can do" attitude. This attitude prompts patients with serious health conditions to believe that they can manage the condition they are coping with, anticipate and address complications, and remember and apply relevant illness- and treatment-related information. Likewise, research demonstrates that **social support** (expressions of care and concern provided by persons within one's circle of family, friends, and colleagues) offers important health benefits for individuals attempting to cope with serious health conditions.

Positive Psychology

Positive psychology represents a positive, philosophical orientation in understanding people and their difficulties. Proponents view individuals as well as their behavioral aberrations through a positive lens that capitalizes on a person's strengths and what he or she can do, rather than focusing on weaknesses and incapacity. For example, treatment efforts often apply a strengths-based approach to resolving clients' difficulties. This approach may involve a fair amount of reframing, which comes down to taking a negative symptom and casting it in a more favorable light. An example of this is reframing a client's complaint about feeling overly stressed at work in a manner that turns the negative symptom into evidence that the client is extremely conscientious. Understanding the problem in this positive light allows an intervention that builds on strength; the client can use the strength to alleviate the negative symptom by learning to be conscientious about leaving work promptly at day's end.

Like some health psychologists, advocates of positive psychology also investigate **subjective well-being**, which is a feeling of general health, vigor, and happiness. Research demonstrates that subjective well-being varies within and across populations worldwide. Because it appears to serve as an indicator (marker) for mental health, psychologists work to ascertain which factors contribute to it and sustain it.

Patients' Rights

Ethical standards and state laws governing the practice of psychology protect the rights of individuals who receive psychological services. One of the most important of these rights is **confidentiality**, an ethical principle that requires psychologists not to disclose information that a patient shares during therapy to others. It must be noted, however, that confidential treatment of communication between a patient and a client is not absolute. Psychologists must discuss the **limits of confidentiality** with patients at the outset of the therapeutic relationship. These limits apply to certain specific circumstances that allow (and sometimes require) psychologists to breach confidentiality.

One situation in which this might occur is when a patient reveals information indicating that he or she intends to harm others or to harm him- or herself. The psychologist must assess the degree of risk by evaluating the seriousness of the threat. For example, many people use expressions such as "I could kill him," "I'm gonna kill her," or "I just want to die," to communicate frustration or anger with another person or with oneself. Psychologists must work to discern whether such statements are truly innocuous or whether the client is expressing a real intent to inflict harm on others or to harm oneself. A psychologist who determines that a client poses a substantial risk of harm to others or to self, incurs a **duty to warn**. This duty obligates the psychologist to inform a fairly broad array of persons and agencies about the potential danger. Laws governing precisely who must be informed in such situations vary from state to state but, in general, these laws work to ensure the safety of the patient *and* any other party who may be at risk. Many states require psychologists to inform law enforcement agencies (e.g., police or domestic abuse agencies), immediate family members (in the case of risk of self-harm), medical agencies (e.g., emergency room personnel), and the party or parties whom the patient intends to harm.

Realistically, it is impossible to warn other people that they are at risk of harm if their identities are unknown. For example, a patient who threatens to harm "the next person who cuts him (or her) off in traffic" has not provided enough information to make a warning feasible. On the other hand, a patient who threatens to harm "one of the regulars at the B&B Bar" has substantially narrowed down the identity of the person potentially at risk. With some further investigation, the specific "regulars" at the B&B Bar can be identified by name and warned of the potential danger.

Thus far, we have addressed confidentiality in the context of an ethical mandate. But this principle also has a legal counterpart—privilege. In its legal sense, **privilege** refers to the rights ensuring individuals that what they communicate to certain specific other individuals will remain private. For example, communications with one's attorney, physician, and psychologist are not subject to disclosure except under highly specific conditions or if a patient (or client) chooses to surrender this right (i.e. waives privilege). In addition to privileged communication, patients have other basic rights including the right to receive treatment as well as the right to refuse treatment. Again, some limits apply. For example, a person who threatens others and thus poses a serious risk of harm to others can be hospitalized for a period of time (often 72 hours) against his or her will. Although such action temporarily restricts the freedom of one person, it can ultimately protect the life of another.

An important legal case served as a bridge between the legal concept of privilege and the psychologically relevant principle of confidentiality. The **Tarasoff ruling** established important precedents for understanding the conditions

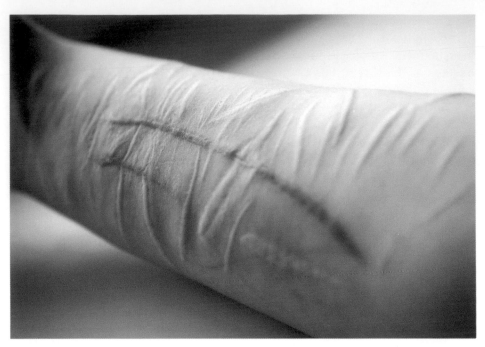

Confidentiality and duty to warn are delicate constructs that sometimes require psychologists to walk a fine line. The bottom line, however, is that no psychologist should ever ignore statements involving a wish to die because the stakes are far too high. Sometimes such statements are expressed in cutting and other forms of self-injury rather than words. The self-injury replaces emotional pain with physical pain, and scars become a reminder of the experience of controlling emotional pain. Self-harming behaviors are not necessarily associated with suicidal intent, but suicide attempts and completions occur with greater frequency among individuals who engage in these behaviors. *(Shutterstock)*

that abridge privilege. This landmark case clarified when confidentiality must be broken and who must be notified when clients make credible threats against others. In this case, a client at a counseling center at a university in California disclosed to the therapist his intent to kill a woman who had rebuffed him, Tatiana Tarasoff. The counselor contacted his supervisor and together they questioned the client about his plans. The client assured them that he would not harm Ms. Tarasoff and was permitted to leave the university grounds. The client later went to Ms. Tarasoff's home and killed her. Her family filed a wrongful death suit against the university. In the end, the court ruled that the counselor's warnings had not gone far enough because the intended victim received no warning. Had she known of the client's intentions, Ms. Tarasoff may have been able to take actions to protect herself from harm. The outcome of the Tarasoff case in California established the duty to warn standard that has been widely adopted in other states.

PSYCHOLOGY IN THE MEDIA

Many people are curious about psychological phenomena especially when these phenomena surface somewhat peripherally in everyday life and do not directly impact them. Watching events unfold from a safe physical (and emotional) distance may be quite fascinating, if not always accurate or easy to fathom. Media portrayals of psychological disorders represent a mixed bag of impressions. Movies with themes involving psychological illness may offer a more or less realistic portrayal of a psychological disorder, contrived to follow a specific plot line rather than to present a completely accurate picture of mental illness. And some films perpetuate unfortunate and inaccurate stereotypes about persons with specific types of psychological disorders or conditions.

News stories involving disordered behavior also undergo considerable editing to focus the reports on facts and events more than on the psychological underpinnings of a given story or event. Worse still, sensationalism within the news media works to promote misconceptions that people with mental illnesses pose a much higher risk of danger than do people without mental disorders when, in fact, the overwhelming majority of individuals with mental disorders are not violent. Moreover, persons with severe mental disorders are far more likely—in fact, two and half times as likely as members of the general public—to be victims of violent crimes than perpetrators.

In the Movies

From the vantage point of movie makers, quirky personalities and aberrant behaviors provide rich possibilities for crafting films that captivate audiences. Many successful movies capitalize on subjects about which we have limited understanding and traditionally create "good guys" and "bad guys." The subject matter of personality and abnormal behavior often lends itself to just such an arrangement. Indeed, the interaction of deviant behaviors and innocent personalities form the foundation of movie classics such as *Psycho* and *Silence of the Lambs*. The so-called slasher films (including the *Jason* and *Chuckie* series, among others) also exploit disordered personalities and deranged behaviors.

Horror films notwithstanding, media portrayals of psychological conditions may shed light on otherwise unknown psychological phenomena. And some films do a reasonable job of humanizing afflicted individuals and showing the far reaching impact of psychological disorders on families, friends, and co-workers. Even so, filmmakers and actors answer to a different authority than psychologists who must behave according to the ethical and practice standards of the profession reviewed in Chapter 5. Movie makers take many liberties in telling a particular story simply to please audiences and thus increase profits. Some films actually end up glorifying ethical misconduct on the part of a psychologist, as when the script includes a sexual relationship between a psychologist

Dustin Hoffman (as Raymond Babbitt in *Rain Man*) portrayed a man with autism or, possibly, Asperger's syndrome. Such fictional (or fictionalized) accounts of individuals with psychological disorders may illustrate the basic nature of certain mental illnesses. Ultimately, however, popular films are commercial ventures intended to entertain rather than educate viewers. *(Photofest)*

and a patient or family member of a patient (the respective themes of *Basic Instinct* and *Prince of Tides*).

In the News

News stories that detail criminal actions of disturbed individuals are common-place. In some of these situations, the person who commits the crime meets the diagnostic criteria for a mental disorder—often a serious one. School shootings, campus shootings, workplace shootings, sniper shootings, infanticide, kidnap-pings, sexual abuse cases, and shaken baby cases appear with alarming regu-larity in the newspaper headlines and as lead stories on network news. Most of us can recall quite easily one or more such stories reported within the past few months. Information that surfaces after the heinous act typically reveals a lone shooter with a deeply troubled past and a family background marked by dysfunction.

In certain cases, some sort of motive emerges: revenge for perceived mis-treatment, liberation from the bonds of parenthood, or sexual gratification, for example. In other instances, the event seems to occur somewhat accidentally, as in the case of a normal reaction accelerating and becoming abnormal. A good example of this case is what can occur when frustration that an infant keeps crying grows into rage and a baby is shaken too harshly. In still other situations, a motive probably exists but only the perpetrator appears to know what it is. These are the most perplexing cases because the usual rules of logic and rational behavior do not apply. A case in point is the relatively recent (2001) case of Andrea Yates, a woman who drowned her five children (apparently in a misguided effort to shield them from the devil's grasp and secure their place in heaven).

Yates had been hospitalized for schizophrenia (and also may have met the diagnostic criteria for postpartum psychosis) just prior to killing her children, but was released when the family's health insurance ran out. Her release occurred over the strong objections of her husband who believed that she was in need of continued care. Despite overwhelming evidence of Yates's mental illness, few people sympathized with her. Put simply, most people found her actions incomprehensible and inexcusable, a rather understandable response because most people have little or no experience with such extreme distortions of reality.

Like the vast majority of **not guilty by reason of insanity** (NGRI) pleas, Yates's plea was unsuccessful—she was convicted of murder. Her case was retried when evidence established that a key prosecution witnesses had fabricated a portion of his testimony. Yates's conviction was overturned and she was sent to a psychiatric facility, where she will receive (and require) treatment most likely for many years.

Although the term **insanity** is not meaningful to psychologists, this term is used in legal contexts to designate a state of mind that prevents an individual from behaving in accordance with the law. Several legal tests of insanity exist, and it is up to each state to decide which standard to use within its borders. According to the *Irresistible Impulse Decision (1834)*, a defendant is not criminally responsible for his or her crime if at the time of the crime the defendant had a mental illness that prevented him or her from resisting the impulse to do the wrong thing. The *M'Naghten Rule (1843)* suggests that a defendant is not responsible for a crime if at the time of the crime he or she had a mental illness that impaired reasoning abilities to such an extent that he or she either (a) did not know what he or she was doing at the time of the crime, or (b) did not know that his or her actions were wrong. The *American Law Institute Model Penal Code (1962)* states that a defendant is not responsible for his or her actions if—as a result of a mental illness at the time of the crime—the defendant lacked the capacity to either (a) appreciate the wrongfulness of his or her actions, or (b) conform his or her behavior to the requirements of the law.

As noted in the preceding paragraphs, NGRI pleas seldom meet with success—only about 1 in 4 cases result in a verdict of not guilty by reason of insanity.

Andrea Yates, the mother who drowned her five children in 2001, garnered little sympathy from a public unable to comprehend the gross distortion of reality under which she operated. Her murder conviction was overturned as a result of flawed testimony given by prosecution witness Park Dietz. *(Brett Coomer-Pool/Getty)*

In addition, fewer than 1 percent of individuals who stand accused of criminal offenses enter a plea of not guilty by reason of insanity perhaps, in part, because of the limited success rate of such a plea. Furthermore, individuals convicted of crimes where NGRI pleas were unsuccessful receive harsher sentences on average than those who entered simple (though unsuccessful) not guilty pleas.

Despite the foregoing, many people believe that NGRI pleas represent a kind of scam whereby skillful criminals work the legal system to their advantage. The close scrutiny the media applies to such stories probably promotes and intensifies this belief. One less publicized feature of such cases is what happens when an NGRI plea is successful. In the vast majority of such cases (95 percent or more by most estimates), the defendant is not released but is legally mandated to undergo treatment, which generally takes place at a secure unit within a psychiatric center. Moreover, it is common for such hospitalizations to last longer than the prison sentence that would have been imposed with a conviction. And although conditions have improved greatly over the past several hundred years, psychiatric treatment facilities are not highly desirable places to live for years on end.

ISSUES IN PROFESSIONAL PRACTICE

A number of issues that confront professional practitioners of psychology may have direct bearing on their clinical work. Some of these issues represent ongoing concerns while others represent relatively recent or emerging concerns. For example, as the next edition of the manual used to diagnose mental disorders approaches publication, the appropriateness of classifying mental disorders (let alone the appropriateness of the labels used to do so) remains the subject of debate. Another issue surfaces as a result of the ongoing escalation of health and mental health care costs. As these costs rise, insurance companies increasingly require psychologists to use treatment techniques with proven effectiveness. Nonetheless, psychology's reach continues to expand. Some therapists attempt to address not only the problems individual clients bring to them but also problems created by the context within which clients live (including oppression and power inequities visited upon various groups); other psychologists pursue the legal right to prescribe medication.

Ongoing Concerns with Classification

Despite the widespread use of the *Diagnostic and Statistical Manual of Mental Disorders* (DSM-IV-TR: American Psychiatric Association, 2000), many people object to the classification of mental disorders, arguing that classifying behaviors can lead us to label *people* rather than their *behaviors* and that those labels, once applied, often remain firmly affixed. One related consequence of classification is that labels may stigmatize those who carry them and reduce people to objects. Accordingly, psychologists advocate the use of **person-first language** (e.g., "individuals with schizophrenia" rather than "schizophrenics" or "students with learning disabilities" rather than "learning-disabled students"). Even though the resultant phrases may appear cumbersome, person-first language accurately conveys information about people. As suggested in Chapter 4, people with mental disorders are more than their psychological diagnoses—they are musicians, actors, sports figures, homemakers, physicians, gardeners, hobbyists, scientists, writers, salespeople, bankers, therapists, and many other things.

A classic study undertaken in the early 1970s by David Rosenhan demonstrated how readily clinicians applied labels and how unwilling they were to remove those labels, even in the face of considerable evidence that the labels were inappropriate. Rosenhan's article "On Being Sane in Insane Places" described how he and seven fellow researchers managed to get themselves admitted to psychiatric units by feigning a single symptom—specifically, auditory hallucinations (hearing voices that were not there)—that they reported at the time of admission only. Based on the self-reported symptom, seven of the eight researchers were diagnosed with schizophrenia. Following admission, the researchers did not alter their typical behavior nor did they mention the voices again. While impersonating patients, the researchers behaved like researchers and wrote extensive notes about their experiences. Staff observed their note taking and in one case described it in the hospital chart (e.g., "patient engaged in writing behavior"). All of the researchers were discharged within two months as "in remission."

Another concern with classification systems involves the ongoing evolution of psychologists' comprehension of various mental disorders. The diagnostic conceptualization (and resulting diagnostic criteria) for a number of mental disorders thus end up being substantially revised from one edition of the diagnostic manual to the next. Sometimes the revisions reflect new research findings or new ways of thinking about disorders, which directly affect treatment. For example, the latest version of the manual (DSM-IV-TR) distinguishes between attention deficit disorders where hyperactivity is prominent and those characterized more by inattention. Hyperactivity is associated not only with high levels of physical activity but also with impulsivity. Impulsive acts, like running into the street to retrieve a ball without considering oncoming traffic, can put a person at risk. Thus, it is important to address hyperactivity but only if it is part of the symptom picture. The significance of making this distinction is not only attention to diagnostic specificity—it can also have a positive effect on treatment options because medications commonly used to control hyperactivity have serious side effects.

Some classification changes appear to be influenced by lobbying efforts or other politically motivated actions. One example of this is the likelihood that Asperger's disorder will be recast in the next (i.e., fifth) edition of the DSM, which is scheduled to appear in 2013. Previously classified as a separate disorder, Asperger's disorder is expected to be grouped under autism spectrum disorders. Some advocates for this revision argued that the change will give individuals with the disorder access to special education services.

Another consideration related to the use of classification systems involves the extent to which diagnosticians agree about which specific diagnosis applies to a specific case. In other words, how reliably are the diagnoses contained in the diagnostic manual applied? Do clinicians arrive at the same diagnostic conclusions when presented with the same symptom picture? Many of the diagnostic categories demonstrate good or very good reliability across evaluators. However, some categories (notably, the personality disorders) are far less dependable in terms of producing identical diagnoses, even when clinicians consider identical case descriptions. Grouping personality disorders into clusters that share general characteristics improved the reliability of DSM personality disorder diagnoses (see Chapter 4 for further information). For example, borderline personality disorder and histrionic personality disorder have many symptoms and basic features in common. Both are grouped as "Cluster B" disorders, all of which demonstrate symptoms marked by overly dramatic, erratic, or highly emotional behaviors. Most clusters demonstrate high reliability. In other words, one diagnostician may regard a given symptom picture as indicating a borderline personality disorder and another may see the picture as reflecting a histrionic personality disorder—but both agree that the disorder falls within Cluster B.

Treatment Effectiveness

Several carefully conducted research studies have established that psychotherapy works. Indeed, about 80 percent of individuals who receive treatment for their psychological difficulties report improvement within about 6 months. Given the wide variety of treatment approaches (described in Chapter 5) coupled with the huge number of psychological disorders (described in Chapter 4) for which people might seek treatment, treatment effectiveness also must be considered "brick by brick." In other words, it is important to evaluate how well a specific intervention works to reduce or eliminate symptoms associated with a specific mental disorder. Treatments for which proof of effectiveness exists are called **evidence-based treatments** or **empirically supported interventions** and comprise the way of the future for psychological interventions. This approach has already helped psychologists to specify which treatments are most effective for particular disorders. For example, dialectical behavior therapy—a variant of behavior therapy that includes cognitive (thinking) aspects of behavior as well as elements of Zen Buddhist philosophy—has demonstrated high levels of treatment effectiveness when used with patients with borderline personality disorders and other disorders with severe symptoms (e.g., self-injury).

Another issue of interest to psychologists is what happens if psychological disorders go untreated. Roughly speaking, it appears that the "rule of thirds" applies to untreated mental disorders—one-third improve, one-third decline, and one-third remain unchanged. Improvement without formal treatment may occur in part because people struggle to get better and sometimes succeed. They may (or may not) seek support through support groups or networks and they may (or may not) receive vital social support from family members or friends. It is important to note that such relationships generally assist healing. With time, with or without such support, an affected individual may find ways to understand and control his or her symptoms.

Nobel laureate John Forbes Nash, Jr., struggled with symptoms of paranoid schizophrenia for decades despite periodic hospitalizations, various treatment efforts, and substantial social support. His self-structured coping strategy enabled numerous and often lengthy periods of remission. *(Bob Strong/APF/Getty Images)*

Four Prominent Feminist Philosophies

Liberal feminists believe that gender disparities result from individual and institutional biases. They often use legal means to remedy inequities—for example, seeking equal pay for equal work.

Cultural feminists regard oppression as the result of a systemic undervaluing of women's unique ways of being. At the societal level, women and men have different roles and these roles are valued differently—for example, domestic work, home making, and teaching are primary roles for women and generally are not highly valued within U.S. culture.

Socialist feminists suggest that oppression stems from capitalism that developed within a male-dominated social structure (patriarchy) where those in charge—historically men—determine the value placed on types of work. They use activism to gain an economic edge—for example, seeking equity pay adjustments on a case by case basis.

Radical feminists believe that men's power over women is the source of all oppression and that patriarchy is deeply ingrained in U.S. culture. They attempt to address multiple oppressions arising from class, race, economics, and so forth.

One fascinating example of this phenomenon is the case of John Forbes Nash—recipient of the Nobel Prize in Economics in 1994 and the subject of the film *A Beautiful Mind*, which was based loosely on his life. (The PBS documentary, *A Brilliant Madness*, presents a more accurate account of Nash's life and the 1998 biography authored by Sylvia Nasar, coincidentally entitled *A Beautiful Mind*, traces his life in an authoritative and accurate manner.) By all accounts, Nash was a brilliant mathematician. His struggles with paranoid schizophrenia began when he was about 30 years old and continued for decades thereafter. Periodically, Nash appeared to experience episodes of full or partial remission; from time to time he received treatment. But he never considered himself fully recovered. He explained his ability to function normally was the result of coping strategies he had developed to help him distinguish between actual voices and auditory hallucinations. Once he determined a voice was not real, he ignored it.

Feminist Perspectives and Therapeutic Framework

Feminist approaches to therapy appear to be gaining in popularity, and these approaches differ from traditional perspectives in several important ways. For one thing, feminist perspectives consider the context within which we exist as vital in shaping our behaviors and overall adjustment. The constraints and demands of the social context that surrounds us can inhibit progress toward our pursuits in myriad ways. At the very least, societal ills contribute to poor psychosocial adjustment.

A number of feminist philosophies underlie current feminist thought. Despite some differences across the various feminist philosophies, several points of agreement deserve mention. For one thing, all views recognize that gender inequities exist and form the basis for other societal ills including **oppression.** Philosophers also agree that power is the basis for gender inequality and that the power differential generally favors men.

Although feminist therapies are grounded in feminist theories and philosophies, their utility extends beyond female therapists and female clients. Therapeutic approaches within the feminist framework emphasize universal issues and values. For the most part, therapeutic applications align with humanistic ideals regarding the worth and dignity of human beings. Feminist theorists and therapists stress the importance of people making choices about their own lives **(autonomy)**, and work to promote an individual's capacity for effecting change **(empowerment)** within a social context where political and cultural factors oppress members of certain groups whose views are discounted **(marginalization)** while privileging members of certain other groups. Oppression and **privilege** form the basis for inequity between societal groups in terms of power. The dynamic just described can play out between almost any two groups that can be understood as (a) those who have power, and (b) those who lack power. Anyone on the receiving end of power abuse suffers harmful effects, be they female, male, gay, straight, bisexual, ethnically diverse, physically disabled, mentally disordered, atheist, believers in a faith not rooted in Judeo-Christian traditions, and so on.

Many therapists employ elements of feminist therapies in concert with another more traditional theoretical orientation. A layer of feminist therapy added to another approach often changes the therapeutic relationship somewhat. Feminist approaches work to reduce or eliminate power differentials between therapists and clients, such as those that characterize some other psychotherapeutic approaches. Therapy represents a true collaboration between the two parties, especially concerning goals, direction, and pace of therapy. Thus, the therapist and client discuss and resolve related issues (e.g., modifications to their schedule of meetings) together, taking each party's concerns into account equally.

Practitioners using a feminist framework interweave philosophy with practice and look at the context of clients' lives rather than internal or unconscious elements. Therapy focuses on actual difficulties the client experiences with an eye toward revealing and understanding how societal realities contribute to the problems. They help clients to distinguish between ideas that have been absorbed from the environment and those that represent what the client truly believes to be important and appropriate for his or her own life. Feminist practitioners often present alternative or even provocative views—for example, suggesting that women's relational qualities (e.g., seeking connectedness) comprise strengths. Therapists work to understand clients' stories as narratives and try to guide clients toward an exploration of life experiences that involve oppression. In addition to promoting change at the individual level, therapists encourage clients to work to change societal structures through advocacy and other forms of action-oriented involvement.

Prescription Privileges

People with some knowledge of the professions might describe the main difference between psychologists and psychiatrists by pointing out that psychiatrists can write prescriptions whereas psychologists cannot. However, this distinction may be on the verge of changing. Two states (New Mexico and Louisiana) already permit psychologists to write prescriptions, and similar legislation is pending in several other states. Typically, psychologists seeking prescription privileges must possess a doctoral degree in psychology (e.g., PhD, PsyD, EdD) and a license to practice and must then undergo additional training through

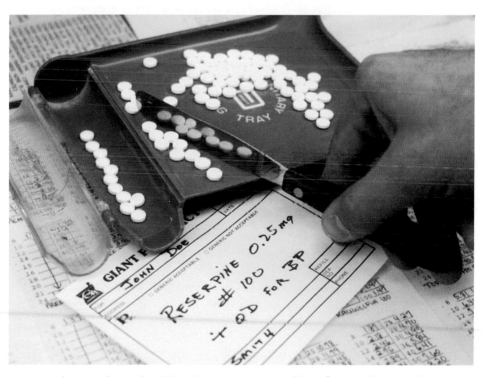

Two states (New Mexico and Louisiana) have already passed laws that permit appropriately trained psychologists to write prescriptions. Prescription privileges may be on the horizon for clinical practitioners of psychology in other states. *(Linda Bartlett. Wikipedia)*

an accredited program. Prescriptive authority for psychologists usually extends only to drugs used to treat psychological disturbances, such as those listed in Chapter 5.

A number of professionals without medical degrees or licenses (for example, physician assistants and nurse practitioners) are permitted to write prescriptions in virtually every state. But although prescription privileges for psychologists have been in place in New Mexico and Louisiana for almost a decade, little research exists to document the worth or impact of psychologists in these states writing prescriptions. Other states have proposed similar legislation and some may be moving toward implementation, but progress on this front has been halting and slow.

CONCLUSION
Like other scientific disciplines, psychological inquiry journeys on and its findings inform the field, among researchers and practitioners alike. As our understanding of behavior and mental processes evolve, various concerns arise while other issues resurface and receive renewed attention. Several topics of special interest as well as issues and concerns bearing on personality and abnormal psychology were addressed in this chapter in an effort to prepare readers for future experience and inquiry within these areas of psychology.

Further Reading

Duckworth, A.L., T.A. Steen, and M.E.P. Seligman. "Positive Psychology in Clinical Practice." *Annual Review of Clinical Psychology* 1 (2005): 629–651.

Gilbert, L.A., and J. Rader. "Feminist Counseling." In A.B. Rochlen (Ed.) *Applying Counseling Theories* (pp. 225-238). Upper Saddle River, N.J.: Pearson, 2007.

Holland, J. *Weekends at Bellevue.* New York: Bantam Books, 2009.

Rosenhan, D.L. "On Being Sane in Insane Places." *Science* 179 (1973): 250–258.

SAMHSA's Resource Center to Promote Acceptance, Dignity and Social Inclusion Associated with Mental Health (n.d.). *Violence and Mental Illness.* Available at http://www.stopstigma.samhsa.gov/topic/facts.aspx.

Seligman, M.E.P., and M. Csikszentmihalyi. "Positive Psychology: An Introduction." *American Psychologist* 55 (2000): 5–14.

Szasz, T. S. "The Myth of Mental Illness." *American Psychologist* 15 (1960): 113–118.

GLOSSARY

acquiescence   Response set wherein a test taker selects responses that reflect agreement with test items rather than selecting answers that best reflect his or her true belief, behavior, or attitude.

actualizing tendency   Concept advanced by Carl Rogers, which suggests that all living things strive to grow and develop in healthy ways that optimize positive outcomes.

adaptability   An indicator of a family's overall health that reflects the degree to which a family is flexible, able, and willing to change.

adaptive functioning   Skills needed to support and engage in everyday life activities.

agoraphobia   Anxiety state characterized by unreasonable and excessive anxiety and fear about being in places or situations from which it may be difficult, impossible, or embarrassing to escape, or in which help may not be available.

analytical psychology   Therapeutic approach advocated by Carl Jung, which emphasizes integration of elements of personality, some of which are unconscious.

antipsychotics (also called neuroleptics or major tranquilizers)   Psychotropic drugs used to combat the most disabling psychological conditions and symptoms involving severe distortions of reality.

anxiety hierarchy   List of elements comprising a feared object or action arranged in order of anxiety associated with each component.

archetypal analysis   In analytical psychology, an examination of the presence and prominence of archetypes—inherited, primitive components of the collective unconscious.

assessment   Broad array of activities involving collection, evaluation, and integration of data from multiple sources with an ultimate goal of enhancing decision making.

assessment battery   Group of procedures used to conduct a comprehensive diagnostic testing process, customized to suit the needs of individual clients.

asylums   Dated expression for institutions that house individuals with mental illnesses and sometimes offer treatment.

attachment   Pronounced emotional and social connections and interactions a child demonstrates with other people in his or her world.

autonomy   One of five fundamental ethical principles that guide the science and practice of psychology, which requires psychologists to recognize clients as individuals capable of making decisions in their own best interests.

axes   In the context of psychiatric diagnoses, dimensions or components used to describe and understand an individual's difficulties and likelihood of recovery.

behavior modification   Behavioral technique that uses operant conditioning (learning) principles to manipulate the consequences of behavior in order to encourage (reinforce) desirable behaviors or discourage (punish) unwanted behaviors.

beneficence   One of five fundamental ethical principles that guide the science and practice of psychology, which requires psychologists to work to promote good outcomes for individuals with whom they work.

biologically based explanation   Reason or description of results or events that depends on physical or physiological states or mechanisms.

biopsychosocial   Framework used within health psychology, which recognizes the importance of biological (physical), psychological (mental), and social factors in shaping overall health.

cardinal traits   One of three types of traits proposed by Gordon Allport, which represent highly salient, singular, or defining characteristics of an individual.

catharsis   Release of pent-up emotions that provides an experience of relief.

central traits   One of three types of traits proposed by Gordon Allport, which represent primary qualities of an individual.

classical learning   A form of associative learning wherein a neutral environmental event (stimulus) occurs repeatedly at the same time as a naturally occurring behavior and establishes an association between the behavior and the event such that the neutral event brings about the behavior.

cognitive triad of depression   Three-part disturbance in thinking often observed in individuals who are depressed—specifically that they are worthless, the world is unjust, and the future is without hope.

cognitive-behavioral therapy   Treatment approach that uses behavioral principles to establish new associations to or new consequences of maladaptive thoughts.

cohesion   An indicator of a family's overall health that reflects the degree of engagement or emotional bonding between and among family members.

collective unconscious   One of three components of personality proposed by Carl Jung, it comprises a deeper, culturally determined level of personality transmitted from our ancestors.

competing response   In behavioral treatment, a state or action that cannot co-occur with another specific state or action.

compulsions   Repetitive overt or covert (mental) acts that one is unable to resist.

conditional positive regard   Represents a "strings attached" form of positive regard whereby positive regard is given only when certain behaviors are demonstrated.

conditions of worth   Circumstances that must exist in order for an individual to receive positive regard, which may lead to alienation from one's true feelings.

confidentiality   Ethical principle that obligates psychologists to maintain the privacy of information shared by patients in the course of therapy.

congruence   An important component of person-centered therapy in which the therapist demonstrates genuineness in his or her interactions with the client.

conscience   In Freudian theory, a part of the superego that generates guilt when we behave in morally inappropriate ways.

construct validity   Evidence that supports the use of test scores in the manner claimed by the test author or publisher where such evidence accrues from several sources.

covert behaviors   Actions that are not readily apparent to others and which take place in one's mind.

deep muscle relaxation   State of extreme and sustained relaxation that extends to all parts of the body and is associated with a calm mental state.

defense mechanisms   In Freudian theory, mostly unconscious techniques employed by the ego to counter anxiety; defenses reduce anxiety by masking its source.

deficit needs   Portion of Abraham Maslow's hierarchy of needs reflecting the most basic, largely physical needs that, when unmet, create a sense of deprivation.

deinstitutionalization   A movement that began in the 1960s and encouraged discharging to the community psychiatric patients many of whom had been hospitalized for years.

delusions   Disturbing cognitive experiences such as beliefs that have no basis in reality, typically involving severe distortion or misinterpretation of innocuous events.

deviance   Response set wherein a test taker selects responses that reflect the highest level of deviance rather than the answer that best reflects his or her true belief, behavior, or attitude.

Diagnostic and Statistical Manual of Mental Disorders   Primary classification system used to render psychiatric diagnoses in the United States, currently in its fourth edition.

differential diagnosis   Part of the process of pinpointing a disorder by highlighting specific features that distinguish the disorder from other related disorders.

duty to warn   Obligation a psychologist incurs to inform (warn) persons who are the intended targets of harm, based on a patient's disclosures within therapy.

echolalia   Symptom associated with autism in which an individual repeats a word or phrase he or she just heard, often in a lilting, noncommunicative fashion.

ego   One of three components of personality proposed by Sigmund Freud, it is mostly unconscious and represents a rational counterpart to the irrational and demanding id; one of three components of personality proposed by Carl Jung, it consists of current thoughts, feelings, and reflections.

ego-ideal   In Freudian theory, a part of the superego that motivates us to behave in morally appropriate ways.

ego-syntonic   Feelings, perceptions, interpretations, and behaviors that one finds agreeable in oneself, even when they are regarded as problematic by others.

empathic understanding   An important component of person-centered therapy in which the therapist demonstrates compassion and sympathy for the client's feelings.

empirical approach   Process used to gather data or evidence firsthand through observation and description.

empirically supported interventions (also called evidence-based treatments)   Treatments for which proof of effectiveness has been demonstrated.

empowerment   Action or state of being in which an individual or group of individuals experiences an increased sense of capacity for effecting change.

erogenous zone   In Freudian theory, the specific part of the body associated with each stage of psychosexual development through which pleasure is derived.

evidence-based treatments (also called empirically supported interventions)   Interventions for which proof of effectiveness has been demonstrated.

expectancies   A social cognitive phenomenon advanced by Julian Rotter, it suggests that if one expects a given behavior to lead to a positive outcome, one will be more likely to engage in that behavior.

external reinforcement   Social cognitive learning concept that refers to an overt consequence of a demonstrated behavior that is initially learned through observation.

extraversion   One of three basic dimensions of personality identified by Hans Eysenck, it refers to one's degree of sociability.

factor analysis   Statistical technique that uses numerical evidence of association among traits to reduce the total number of possible traits to a smaller, more meaningful number.

false negative   Type of test error in which test results suggest the absence of a particular condition or symptom that in fact exists.

false positive   Type of test error in which test results suggest the presence of a particular condition or symptom that in fact does not exist.

feelings of inferiority   According to Alfred Adler, the sense that we have of ourselves as less than perfect and incomplete.

fidelity   One of five fundamental ethical principles that guide the science and practice of psychology, it requires psychologists to be trustworthy and reliable.

five-factor model   A popular and influential trait theory that posits five key personality traits, namely openness to experience, conscientiousness, extraversion, agreeableness, and neuroticism.

fixations   In Freudian theory, leftover conflicts that result from failing to pass completely through certain psychosexual stages and that continue to consume psychic energy; they are thematically linked to the stage in which they first appeared.

free association   Psychoanalytic treatment technique wherein a client reports immediately every thought that enters his or her mind without blocking (censoring) any content.

Freudian slips   Errant utterances that psychodynamically oriented theorists suggest provide evidence of unconscious but powerful elements of personality.

generalize   To apply or extend a learned behavioral response in situations similar to the one in which the behavior was initially acquired.

genogram   Graphic representation of family structure extending across three or more generations, which captures information about members and relationships among them.

gestalt therapy   Treatment approach aligned with the general principles of a humanistic orientation that emphasizes the importance of fully experiencing each moment of one's current situation.

growth needs   Portion of Abraham Maslow's hierarchy of needs reflecting higher levels of needs that are psychological in nature and that, when met, contributes to personal growth and fulfillment.

hallucinations   Disturbing sensory experiences that are not grounded in reality and occur only in an individual sufferer's mind.

health psychology   Relatively new field of psychology, which recognizes several factors that influence both physical and mental health as well as the interaction between these factors.

hierarchy of needs   Explanation of human motivation proposed by Abraham Maslow and suggesting that people seek to meet their needs in a specific order beginning with basic needs and progressing to higher level needs such as self-esteem needs.

high-stakes decisions   Weighty decisions with substantial impacts on individual lives.

humors   Fluids contained in the body—specifically blood, black bile, yellow bile, and phlegm—the balance among which Hippocrates believed affected temperament (personality).

id   One of three components of personality proposed by Sigmund Freud, it is entirely unconscious and represents the most primitive aspect of personality consisting of raw, inborn, illogical, unorganized urges, wants, impulses, drives, and cravings.

identified patient   In the context of family therapy, family member whom other members regard as the "one" with the problem.

imitation (also called observational learning, social modeling, vicarious learning)   Action of repeating behavior that one observes another person perform; the observed behavior becomes established in (learned by) the observer.

incongruity   An unhealthy state marked by lack of agreement between who one truly is, based on one's actual behaviors, and the person one aspires to be.

individual psychology   Therapeutic approach advocated by Alfred Adler, which emphasizes education as therapists help clients understand how early life experiences have shaped their personalities.

individuation   Process within analytical psychology, which marks the emergence of a cohesive sense of self that integrates disparate aspects of one's identity.

inferiority complex   According to Alfred Adler, ongoing concern generated by failure to achieve one's tasks and goals.

inquiry   Second phase of administration of tests such as the Rorschach inkblots wherein test takers explain and describe their original responses.

insanity   Legal term used to describe a state of mind that prevents an individual from behaving in accordance with the law.

insight   Awareness and understanding of one's own motivations for particular feelings and behaviors.

intelligence   Capacity to understand the world, think rationally, and use resources effectively when faced with challenges.

internal consistency reliability   Property of a test that indicates the degree to which the test's items are consistent with one another and thereby work in a unified manner to assess a specific construct.

International Classification of Diseases   Primary classification system used to render medical and psychiatric diagnoses worldwide, currently in its tenth revision.

interrater reliability (also called interscorer reliability)   Property of a test that indicates the degree to which the test produces the same results when different people score the test.

involuntary commitment   Legal procedures through which individuals may be held against their will in a setting that provides psychiatric treatment.

justice   One of five fundamental ethical principles that guide the science and practice of psychology, it requires equitable, respectful treatment of clients.

latent content   Underlying meaning of a dream; according to psychoanalytic dream interpretation, this content reveals unconscious motivations.

libido   In Freudian theory, the psychic energy that drives all components and aspects of personality.

life goal   According to Alfred Adler, the motivation that helps us to make purposeful choices and inspires us to overcome feelings of inferiority.

lifestyle assessment   Technique used by Adlerian therapists to learn about clients; it includes gathering information about family constellation, birth order, early recollections, and subjective judgments held by clients.

lifestyle patterns   Characteristic ways of behaving when dealing with all life tasks, these develop from early childhood efforts used to navigate life within the family context.

limits of confidentiality   Specific conditions (risk of harm to self or others) under which the confidentiality of information shared between a patient and his or her psychotherapist must be abandoned.

locus of control   Concept initially proposed by Julian Rotter to explain how people differ in their beliefs about whether they control events that impact them or whether events control them.

major depressive episode   Period of 2 weeks or more during which an individual's mood is depressed or there has been a (nearly) complete loss of interest or pleasure in the individual's usual activities; additional criteria must be met.

major tranquilizers (also called antipsychotics or neuroleptics)   Psychotropic drugs used to combat the most disabling conditions and symptoms involving severe distortions of reality.

manic episode   Period of 1 week or more during which an individual's mood is abnormally and persistently elevated, expansive, elated, or irritable, and behavior may become reckless; additional criteria must be met.

manifest content   Surface level description of a dream; according to psychoanalytic dream interpretation, this content is of little use in understanding the unconscious.

marginalization   Action or state of society that discounts or fails to consider or fails to value the views or needs of specific groups within that society.

medical model   View of mental disorders as illnesses that result from biological abnormalities and diseases that should be treated with biologically based practices such as medication.

moral therapy   Humane and supportive approach to treating individuals with mental disorders as normal people who have shouldered unusually heavy burdens.

multi-axial system   Approach to psychiatric diagnosis, which considers more than one dimension of functioning.

neuroleptics (also called antipsychotics or major tranquilizers)   Psychotropic drugs used to combat the most disabling conditions and symptoms involving severe distortions of reality.

neurotic anxiety   In Freudian theory, a common type of tension produced when the ego perceives that the id's unacceptable urges and demands will be met, prompting punishment.

neuroticism   One of three basic dimensions of personality identified by Hans Eysenck, it refers to one's level of emotional stability.

non-maleficence   One of five fundamental ethical principles that guide the science and practice of psychology, it requires psychologists to strive to avoid harming individuals with whom they work.

normal distribution   Frequency plot that is symmetrical and "bell shaped" such that scores near the center of the range occur with greatest frequency and extreme scores are quite infrequent.

not guilty by reason of insanity   Plea entered in a legal proceeding when attorneys for the accused believe the client should not be held responsible for a crime because of mental illness.

objective measures   Tests that lend themselves to automated scoring, either by computer or by hand using a scoring template.

observational learning (also called imitation, social modeling, vicarious learning)   Action of repeating behavior that one observes another person perform; the observed behavior becomes established in (learned by) the observer.

obsessions   Intrusive thoughts, ideas, images, or impulses that recur even though one would rather they did not.

operant learning   A form of consequential learning wherein the likelihood of a given behavior being repeated is affected by environmental events—reinforcements or punishments—that follow the behavior.

oppression   Action or state of society that singles out and suppresses or otherwise disregards a group of individuals purely on the basis of their group membership.

overt behaviors   Actions that are observable by other people.

panic attack   An episode of intense anxiety or fear when no real danger exists; it may signal the presence of an underlying anxiety disorder.

performance-based measures (also known as projective techniques)   Psychological measures that present ambiguous stimuli and ask test takers to make sense of the ambiguity and fashion responses.

persecutory delusions   Severely distorted beliefs that follow a theme of being followed, watched, tormented, bothered, tricked, or ridiculed.

personal unconscious   One of three components of personality proposed by Carl Jung, it consists of stored thoughts, feelings, and memories.

personality   Enduring characteristic demonstrated by individuals, which are stable across time and across a variety of situations.

person-centered treatment   Therapeutic approach advocated by Carl Rogers, which respects the dignity and autonomy of the individual.

person-first language   Style of writing or speaking about individuals with various afflictions, which mentions the individual (e.g., "student") before mentioning his or her illness or disability (e.g., "with a learning disability").

positive psychology   Orientation or philosophical approach to understanding people and their difficulties, which emphasizes strengths and capabilities.

positive regard   Concept advanced by Carl Rogers, which consists of warmth, respect, and acceptance in support of people reaching their full potentials.

priorities (also called typologies)   According to Alfred Adler, one's most favored lifestyle patterns.

private logic   In Adlerian theoretical framework, an individual's unique way of understanding life events.

privilege   Legal counterpart of confidentiality that comprises legal rights held by individuals and specifically protect the privacy of communications with certain individuals, including psychologists; action or state of society that accords advantages to certain groups within that society, thereby creating inequities of power between societal groups.

projective techniques (also called performance-based measures)   Psychological measures that present ambiguous stimuli and ask test takers to make sense of the ambiguity and fashion responses.

psychoanalysis   Classical approach to psychotherapy founded by Sigmund Freud, which involves frequent meetings between the analyst and the patient over an extended period of time.

psychogenic   Originating or arising from the mind or mental processes.

psychopharmaceutical agents (also called psychotropic drugs)   Drugs that affect patients' emotions, cognitions (thoughts), and behaviors and are used specifically to treat psychological disorders.

psychosexual stages   In Freudian theory, the oral, anal, phallic, latency, and genital stages that comprise the series of events through which all people progress and as a result of which personality is formed.

psychotherapy   Psychologically based therapy in which a trained mental health professional engages a patient and applies psychological principles and techniques.

psychotic   Profound disruption of an individual's experience of reality.

psychoticism   One of three basic dimensions of personality identified by Hans Eysenck, it refers to the degree to which one distorts reality.

psychotropic drugs (also called psychopharmaceutical agents)   Drugs that affect patients' emotions, cognitions (thoughts), and behaviors and are used specifically to treat psychological disorders.

reality principle   In Freudian theory, the response style employed by the ego to address the demands of the id by using realistic, safe, and socially acceptable means.

reciprocal determinism   A social cognitive learning concept positing that internal, cognitive events and external, environmental events affect each other.

referential delusions   Severely distorted beliefs that follow a theme of being the target or subject of various comments, newspaper articles, radio shows, songs, newscasts, or book passages.

reframing   Technique often applied in positive psychology wherein a seemingly negative symptom or behavior is cast in a favorable light.

reliability   Property of a test, which indicates the degree to which the test produces dependable results.

resistance   An important component of psychoanalytic treatment, which represents a patient's tendency to slow the pace or otherwise inhibit the progress of therapy.

response sets   Patterned, systematic approaches in which test takers may respond to test items, especially those comprising self-report measures, that produces distortions of test results.

schizophrenia   A psychotic disorder in which there is a profound disruption of one's experience of reality that may be accompanied by pronounced disturbances in thinking and/or perceptual irregularities.

scholastic intelligence   Cognitive ability reflected primarily in school-related activities.

screening measure   Procedure that assesses the likely presence or absence of specific clinical symptoms in order to determine whether further testing is needed.

secondary traits   One of three types of traits proposed by Gordon Allport, these are the least salient trait type and influence behavior only under specific situations.

self-actualization   Natural tendency of individuals to strive toward growth and fulfillment of one's potential, and to be autonomous, self-aware, and healthy.

self-reinforcement   A social cognitive learning concept that refers to a consequence delivered to oneself, by oneself, for demonstrating a particular behavior initially learned through observation.

self-report   Type of test format that relies upon test takers to answer questions; usually presented as a paper and pencil survey or inventory.

semi-structured interview   Process of asking questions about certain areas of an individual's life without using formal procedures or scripted questions.

sensitivity   Quality of a test, which reflects the frequency with which it correctly signals the presence of a condition or symptom.

shadow   According to Carl Jung, the dark nature of our unconscious existence that may be expressed through dreams.

situational specificity   Tendency for personality traits to surface under one set of circumstances and not under other circumstances.

social cognitive approaches   Explanations of personality that build upon the recognition that people learn behaviors within the social context of their environments.

social desirability   Response set wherein a test taker responds to items by endorsing the most socially appropriate responses rather than the answer that best reflects his or her true belief, behavior, or attitude.

social modeling (also called imitation, observational learning, vicarious learning)   Action of repeating behavior that one observes another person perform such that the observed behavior becomes established in (learned by) the observer.

social phobia   Excessive and pronounced fear of social situations in which embarrassment may occur.

social support   Expressions of care and concern provided by persons within one's circle of family, friends, and colleagues.

somatogenic   Originating or arising from bodily structures.

specific phobias   Fears associated with ordinarily benign objects or situations that pose little or no risk to the individual experiencing the fear.

specificity   Quality of a test that reflects the frequency with which it correctly signals the absence of a condition or symptom.

split-half reliability   Type of test reliability derived by dividing test items into two halves and comparing (correlating) performance on the two halves to assess internal consistency.

standardization sample   Group of test takers who, during test development, take the final version of a standardized test just prior to its release.

standardized tests   Measures comprising samples of behavior that require close adherence to specified administration procedures; these are established during the process of test development to ensure that test takers are treated in the same manner.

state anxiety   Tension and worry that exists at a given moment and generally arises in response to specific environmental events.

striving for superiority   According to Alfred Adler, the natural quest to reach one's personal best and to accomplish tasks and goals that one establishes for oneself.

structured interview   Process of asking specific "scripted" questions with standard procedures for recording responses and asking follow-up questions.

subjective distress   Level of stress, dissatisfaction, despair, tension, confusion, fear, and anxiety perceived by an individual as affecting his or her life.

subjective measures   Tests that require some degree of judgment by the person who scores them; such tests cannot be scored using automation.

subjective well-being   Feeling of general health, vigor, and happiness experienced by individuals.

superego   One of three components of personality proposed by Sigmund Freud, it operates primarily on an unconscious level and embodies society's morals as taught primarily by parents and teachers.

systematic desensitization   Behavioral technique often used to treat phobias, which establishes a new association to the feared object or action by pairing elements from a patient-generated anxiety hierarchy with a previously established state of intense relaxation.

systems perspective   Viewpoint that regards (family) functioning in terms of how well the entire unit works, rather than how well individual members of the unit work.

Tarasoff ruling   Landmark legal case that established precedents for understanding the conditions under which confidentiality must be abridged as well as who, specifically, must be notified when clients make credible threats against other individuals.

tardive dyskinesia   Severe side effects of psychotropic drugs; these include any of a large group of involuntary muscle movements generally consisting of repetitive and purposeless movements often involving facial muscles.

test   Sample of a specific behavior or characteristic, taken at a particular point in time, under particular circumstances.

test norms   Standards of test performance that form the basis for comparison of scores obtained by actual test takers.

test-retest reliability   Property of a test that indicates the degree to which the test produces the same results across a specific interval of time.

tics   Mostly involuntary, sudden, and recurrent motor movements (typically facial) or vocalizations.

token economy   Variant of behavior modification; involves rewarding desired behaviors with symbolic markers that may be redeemed later for desired items or privileges.

tolerance   Physiological process that occurs when a substance user requires greater and greater amounts of the substance to achieve a desired effect.

trait anxiety   Tension and worry that surface routinely in response to various environmental events, signifying anxiety proneness.

traits   Dimensions of personality, of which there are a finite number.

transference   An important component of psychoanalytic treatment, it describes a patient's tendency to relate to the analyst in a way that mirrors his or her interactions with significant others from the past.

trephining   Procedure of drilling a hole into the skull of living person, possibly used in ancient times to release evil spirits from the brain.

typologies (also called priorities)   According to Alfred Adler, one's most favored lifestyle patterns.

unconditional positive regard   A "no strings attached" form of positive regard in which positive regard is not linked to specific behaviors or conditions.

validity   Property of test scores that indicates the degree to which the scores accurately reflect the behavior or characteristic the test purportedly measures.

validity scales   Measures included on many psychological tests built to detect response sets that reveal a test taker is answering questions in certain patterns rather than truthfully.

vicarious learning (also called imitation, observational learning)   The action of repeating behavior that one observes another person perform such that the observed behavior becomes established in (learned by) the observer.

vicarious reinforcement   Social cognitive learning concept that refers to an indirect experience of reinforcement, such as that which occurs when an observer watches a model receive a consequence for demonstrating a particular behavior.

withdrawal   Physiological process that produces specific symptoms following the cessation of use of a particular substance.

BIBLIOGRAPHY

American Association of Suicidology. Available at http://www.suicidology.org.

American Psychological Association. "Ethical Principles of Psychologists and Code of Conduct." *American Psychologist* 57 (2002): 1060–1073.

American Psychological Association. Record Keeping Guidelines: Drafted by the Committee on Professional Practice & Standards, a committee of the Board of Professional Affairs, adopted by the Council of Representatives, February 2007. Available at http://www.apa.org/practice/recordkeeping.html.

American Psychological Association. Ethical Principles of Psychologists and Code of Conduct. (2010 Amendments). Available at www.apa.org/ethics.

Anastasi, A., and S. Urbina. *Psychological Testing*. 7th ed. Upper Saddle River, N.J.: Prentice Hall, 1997.

Bandura, A. "Social Cognitive Theory: An Agentic Perspective." *Annual Review of Psychology* 52 (2001): 1–52.

Baur, S. *The Dinosaur Man: Tales of Madness and Enchantment from the Back Ward*. New York: HarperCollins, 1991.

Beck, A. "The Development of Depression: A Cognitive Model." In T. Millon (Ed.), Theories of Personality. 3rd ed. (pp. 247–256). New York: Holt, Rinehart, & Winston, 1983.

Bernard, J. M. "Life Lines—Laura Perls: From Ground to Figure." *Journal of Counseling and Development* 64 (1986): 367–374.

Chodoff, P. "Psychiatric Diagnosis: A 60-year Perspective." *Psychiatric News* 40 (June 2005): 17.

Duckworth, A.L., T. A. Steen, and M.E.P. Seligman. "Positive Psychology in Clinical Practice." *Annual Review of Clinical Psychology* 1 (2005): 629–651.

Ellis, A. "Addictive Behaviors and Personality Disorders." *Social Policy* 29 (1998): 25–30.

FAQ/Finding Information About Psychological Tests. Available at http://www .apa.org/science/programs/testing/find-tests.aspx#.

Frequently Asked Questions About DSM. Available at http://www.psych.org/ MainMenu/Research/DSMIV/FAQs.aspx.

Friedman, H.S., and M.W. Schustrack. *Readings in Personality: Classic Theorists and Modern Research.* Boston: Allyn & Bacon, 2001.

Genova, L. *Still Alice.* New York: Pocket Books, 2009.

Gilbert, L.A., and J. Rader. "Feminist Counseling." In A.B. Rochlen (Ed.), *Applying Counseling Theories* (pp. 225–238). Upper Saddle River, N.J.: Pearson, 2007.

Halbur, D.A., and K. Vess Halbur. *Developing Your Theoretical Orientation in Counseling and Psychotherapy.* 2nd ed. Upper Saddle River, N.J.: Pearson Education, 2011.

Henle, M. "Gestalt Psychology and Gestalt Therapy." *Journal of the History of the Behavioral Sciences* 14 (1978): 23–32.

Holland, J. *Weekends at Bellevue.* New York: Bantam Books, 2009.

Hood, A.B., and R.W. Johnson. *Assessment in Counseling: A Guide to the Use of Psychological Assessment Procedures.* 4th ed. Alexandria, Va.: American Counseling Association, 2007.

Joint Committee on Testing Practices (JCTP). *Rights and Responsibilities of Test Takers: Guidelines and Expectations.* Washington, D.C.: Author, 1999. Available at http://www.apa.org/science/ttrr.html.

Kelly, E.W., Jr. "Relationship-centered Counseling: A Humanistic Model of Integration." *Journal of Counseling and Development* 75 (1997): 337–345.

Lilienfeld, S.O., J.M. Wood, and H.N. Garb. "The Scientific Status of Projective Techniques." *Psychological Science in the Public Interest* 1 (2000): 27–66.

Maruish, M.E. *The Use of Psychological Testing for Treatment Planning and Outcomes Assessment.* 2nd ed. Mahwah, N.J.: Erlbaum, 1999.

Maslow, A.H. "Some Basic Propositions of a Growth and Self-actualization Psychology." In *Toward a Psychology of Being* (pp. 189–214). New York: Von Nostrund, 1962. Available at http://psychclassics.yorku.ca/Maslow/ motivation.htm.

Mitchell, S.A., and M.J. Black. *Freud and Beyond: A History of Modern Psychoanalytic Thought.* New York: Basic Books, 1995.

Mosak, H.H., and M.P. Maniacci. *Primer of Adlerian Psychology.* New York: Brunner/Routledge, 1999.

Preston, J.D., J.H. O'Neal, and M.C. Talaga. *Consumer's Guide to Psychiatric Drugs.* New York: Simon & Schuster, 2009.

Quick Reference to Psychotropic Medication (2009 update). Available from: http://www.psyd-fx.com/html/quick_reference_chart.html.

Roberts, B.W., and W.F. DelVecchio. "The Rank-order Consistency of Personality Traits from Childhood to Old Age: A Quantitative Review of Longitudinal Studies. *Psychological Bulletin* 126 (2000): 3–25.

Rock, I., and S. Palmer. "The Legacy of Gestalt Psychology." *Scientific American* 263, no. 6 (1990): 84–90.

Rogers, C.R. *A Way of Being.* Boston: Houghton-Mifflin, 1980.

Rosenhan, D.L. "On Being Sane in Insane Places." *Science* 179 (1973): 250–258.

Sacks, O. *The Man Who Mistook His Wife for a Hat and Other Clinical Tales.* New York: HarperCollins, 1985.

SAMHSA's Resource Center to Promote Acceptance, Dignity and Social Inclusion Associated with Mental Health (n.d.). Violence and mental illness. Available at http://www.stopstigma.samhsa.gov/topic/facts.aspx.

Schultz, D., and S.E. Schultz. *Theories of Personality.* 8th ed. Pacific Grove, Calif.: Brooks/Cole, 2005.

Seligman, M.E.P. "The Effectiveness of Psychotherapy: The Consumer's Report Study." *American Psychologist* 50 (1995): 965–974.

Seligman, M.E.P., and M. Csikszentmihalyi. "Positive Psychology: An Introduction." *American Psychologist* 55 (2000): 5–14.

Spitzer, R.L., and M.B. First. "Classification of Psychiatric Disorders." *Journal of the American Medical Association* 294 (2005): 1898–1899.

Szasz, T.S. "The Myth of Mental Illness." *American Psychologist* 15 (1960): 113–118.

Watson, J., and R. Rayner. "Conditioned Emotional Reactions." *Journal of Experimental Psychology* 3 (1920): 1–14.

Widiger, T.A., and L. M. Sankis. "Adult Psychopathology: Issues and Controversies." *Annual Review of Psychology* 51 (2000): 377–404.

INDEX

Note: Page numbers followed by *g* indicate glossary entries.

A

abnormal behavior 23–41. *See also* mental
  disorders
  biological explanations of 33–34, 36, 37
  in children 66–71, 97, 98
  defining 23–29
  as deviation from average 23–24
  as deviation from ideal 24–26
  feminist theory on 119–120
  Hippocrates on 31–34
  historical views of 30–37
  humanistic theory on 38–39, 91
  as inability to function effectively 27–29
  learning theory on 37 38
  psychodynamic theory on 40
  and subjective distress 26, 38–39, 63
  trait theory on 37
acquiescence 55, 123*g*
actualizing tendency 12, 123*g*
adaptability (of family) 99, 123*g*
adaptive functioning 69, 123*g*
Adler, Alfred 20–21
  individual psychology 94–95, 96, 129*g*
  inferiority complex 40, 129*g*
  personality theory 20, 94–95
adolescence, mental disorders in 66–71
aerophobia 86–87

agoraphobia 74–75, 123*g*
Allport, Gordon 4
American Counseling Association (ACA)
  100
American Law Institute Model Penal Code
  (1962) 113
American Psychological Association (APA),
  ethics and professional conduct code of
  100, 101, 102
analytical psychology 94, 123*g*
ancient societies 30, 31
antipsychotics 82 83, 123*g*
antisocial personality disorder 72
anxiety
  defense mechanisms against 19, 20, 40,
    126*g*
  moral 19
  neurotic 19, 131*g*
  normal v. abnormal 73–74
  psychodynamic theory on 18–19
  reality 19
  screening measures for 61
  state 61, 135*g*
  trait 61, 136*g*
anxiety disorders 73–76, 81
anxiety hierarchy 86, 123*g*
archetypal analysis 94, 124*g*